M000025007

High
impact
speeches

Books to make you better

Books to make you better. To make you *be* better, *do* better, *feel* better. Whether you want to upgrade your personal skills or change your job, whether you want to improve your managerial style, become a more powerful communicator, or be stimulated and inspired as you work.

Prentice Hall Business is leading the field with a new breed of skills, careers and development books. Books that are a cut above the mainstream – in topic, content and delivery – with an edge and verve that will make you better, with less effort.

Books that are as sharp and smart as you are.

Prentice Hall Business.
We work harder – so you don't have to.

For more details on products, and to contact us, visit
www.business-minds.com
www.yourmomentum.com

RICHARD HELLER

High impact speeches

How to create and deliver words that move minds

Prentice
Hall

BUSINESS

An imprint of Pearson Education

London • New York • Toronto • Sydney • Tokyo • Singapore • Hong Kong • Cape Town
New Delhi • Madrid • Paris • Amsterdam • Munich • Milan • Stockholm

Pearson Education Limited

Edinburgh Gate
Harlow CM20 2JE
Tel: +44 (0) 1279 623623
Fax: +44 (0) 1279 431059
Website: www.pearsoned.co.uk

First published in Great Britain in 2003

© Pearson Education Limited 2003

The right of Richard Heller to be identified as Author of this Work has been
asserted by him in accordance with the Copyright, Designs and Patents Act 1988.
ISBN-10: 0-273-66202-3

ISBN-13: 978-0-273-66202-0
British Library Cataloguing in Publication Data
A CIP catalogue record for this book can be obtained from the British Library

All rights reserved; no part of this publication may be reproduced, stored in a
retrieval system, or transmitted in any form or by any means, electronic,
mechanical, photocopying, recording, or otherwise without either the prior written
permission of the Publishers or a licence permitting restricted copying in the
United Kingdom issued by the Copyright Licensing Agency Ltd, 90 Tottenham Court
Road, London W1T 4LP. This book may not be lent, resold, hired out or
otherwise disposed of by way of trade in any form of binding or cover other than
that in which it is published, without the prior consent of the Publishers.

10 9 8 7 6 5 4

Typeset by Northern Phototypesetting Co. Ltd, Bolton
Printed and bound in Great Britain by Bell & Bain Ltd, Glasgow

The Publishers' policy is to use paper manufactured from sustainable forests.

Contents

Introduction

'I'm making a speech!'

'I'm speaking prose! I'm speaking prose!' says M. Jourdain, the hero of Molière's *Le Bourgeois Gentilhomme*. In this seventeenth-century satire, a newly-rich businessman decides that he needs social polish and employs an army of tutors. In his speech lesson, his voice tutor tells him that he can speak either prose or verse; anything which is not verse must be prose. His pupil is delighted to discover he has been speaking prose all his life.

Today's M. Jourdain might well exclaim: 'I'm making a speech! I'm making a speech!' His tutor might tell him that every word he communicates must be either written or spoken; anything which is not written must be a speech.

Speech-making at its simplest means communicating something by the spoken word. 'On your marks . . . Get set . . . Go!' is a speech. So is 'What's the time?' or 'Big Mac with large fries, please.' The least communicative people on earth, male teenagers, are speech-makers. After 'Where are you going?' their grunted, over-the-shoulder reply 'Out' is still a speech.

Narrow the definition and think of a 'speech' as an organized body of words in some kind of formal setting to an audience which is expected to listen. Even on this more conventional definition the world is full of speeches and speech-makers.

In one of his more memorable speeches, Richard Nixon coined the phrase 'the silent majority'. He was wrong. The majority is not silent: almost everyone is a public speaker. In fact, it is very hard to get through life without having to make some kind of formal speech. If you get married, if you have children, if you give a toast or a vote of thanks or graciously accept an award, if you teach any kind of class, if you ever want people to vote for you or support a cause, if you ever represent your business or your organization at a formal gathering, if you ever become any kind of leader, you will find yourself in front of an audience with nothing more to rely on than the power of your words. And if you are lucky enough to miss all these demands for a speech – they will still get you on your retirement.

Sometime, somewhere you are going to be a public speaker.

Sometime, somewhere you are going to be a public speaker. This book will help you to do it well. It will give you methods and tools for creating speeches which produce *your chosen result* – speeches which entertain, speeches which inform, speeches which persuade, speeches which make news – or make money, speeches which advance your career, speeches which make the audience invite you back next year . . . In three words, *High Impact Speeches*.

New rewards for high impact speaking

Modern life is turning more and more people into public speakers. It is also offering them greater rewards for doing it well. It seems like a paradox. Modern technology offers more and more different methods of delivering a message and yet there is a new demand for the oldest method of all: live speech.

I think this reflects a big change in global society. For centuries, people lived apart from each other, separated by nationality, by occupation, by social status, by race, by gender. English people spoke mostly to other English people, merchants spoke mostly to other merchants; except for the purpose of giving orders, landowners spoke mostly to other landowners and white people mostly to other white people. Men spoke mostly to other men, women spoke mostly to other women. The United States was the first society to grow up without these barriers (except those of race): Americans talked to each other more than any other country, and they still do. It is one of the factors which made the United States a dynamic society and the most successful economy in history.

Modern life is turning more and more people into public speakers.

The world has learnt to follow the United States. Everybody speaks to everybody, and people explain themselves to other people. There is a continuous dialogue between nations and between different interest groups: businesses talk to government, to employees, to customers, to pressure groups and to their competitors. Governments talk to other governments and to their own citizens and voters. Special interest groups talk constantly to allies and adversaries. Voluntary groups talk to citizens, and businesses, and governments and to each other.

All of these overlapping dialogues generate public meetings and public speaking.

Everybody speaks to everybody, and people explain themselves to other people.

In the business world it is no longer enough for executives to be good at making things or selling them or keeping costs down or delivering shareholder value. They are also expected to explain things and persuade people to do things in meetings, both external and internal. They have to talk to many different audiences. Crafting good speeches has become an essential business skill and a component of a successful career.

The same is true of officials in national and local government. They no longer rule us silently and anonymously, and we expect them to speak to us regularly.

For charities and voluntary bodies, there is a very practical need for public speaking: raising funds. Good speeches mean more money for good causes, whether it is the extra coin on the collection plate or winning over the big corporate sponsor.

In fact, organizations of every kind are faced with more and more demands and opportunities to speak to an outside audience on a set occasion. Within organizations, both in business and in the public and voluntary sectors, the growth of committees and formal internal meetings and consultation processes is turning more and more employees into public speakers. *Because of these changes more and more leaders and managers in all organizations expect other people to draft speeches for them.*

That is why this book gives advice on how to produce **High Impact Speeches** for somebody else.

If business and government and other organizations spend more time in public meetings, so too does the general public. People often find themselves having to persuade an audience, whether it is a mass meeting or in a small deputation to a local official. More and more people are doing some kind of public or voluntary service – councillors, school governors, in faith groups, charities and community organizations, on the committee to save their local school. All of this kind of work means more meetings and more speaking. More and more people are giving classes or lectures of some kind, or becoming guest speakers at clubs and societies.

For everybody without exception, a good speech is a good career move (even if it is delivered by someone else).

All of these new demands for public speaking offer new rewards. In business a good speech can change perceptions of a company, head off demands for regulation, turn sceptics and enemies into customers or shareholders. In government a good speech wins votes, for pressure groups a good speech creates the right kind of pressure, for voluntary bodies and charities a good speech wins volunteers and contributions. For citizens' groups, a good speech can actually save the local school. For the willing amateur, a good speech means more invitations.

For everybody without exception, a good speech is a good career move (even if it is delivered by someone else).

The revival of rhetoric

For all of these reasons, we are seeing a revival of rhetoric: the art of speaking.

In classical times, rhetoric was one of the seven liberal arts, and for over two thousand years no man could call himself educated or command a place in society unless he had mastered the arts of speaking in public and moving an audience. (Women, of course, were not encouraged to speak or even form part of the audience.)

For Plato and Aristotle, who could be called its founders, rhetoric meant much more than being skilful in the use of words. It had a strong social and ethical dimension. It was one of the 'liberal' arts – which defined a free citizen – rather than the productive and industrial arts which were used by slaves. By learning rhetoric, men learnt to be judges, lawgivers and leaders, and to fulfil their potential for excellence.

For Aristotle rhetoric was 'the faculty of discovering in any given case the available means of persuasion'. It taught men how to find the truth, how to cultivate and engage with other men, and how to persuade them of the truth. For Aristotle, a good speech rested on three pillars: accuracy, pleasure and argument. Its facts should be indisputable, its choice of words enjoyable, its logic inescapable.

In the Christian era, rhetoric acquired a new moral purpose: converting people and persuading them to accept the word of God. In the Renaissance era, rhetoric became associated with two secular faiths: the law and representative politics. It was an essential skill for winning a case in the law courts and winning a majority in parliament or the council chamber.

However, by the nineteenth century, rhetoric had lost these fine associations and become a derogatory term, with overtones of facile, flashy and false. In that way it was used in one of the most memorable speeches of all time: the scientist T. H. Huxley in 1860, defending Charles Darwin's theory of evolution in a public meeting against Bishop 'Soapy Sam' Wilberforce:

❝I asserted – and I repeat – that a man has no reason to be ashamed of having an ape for his grandfather. If there were an ancestor whom I should feel shame in recalling it would rather be a *man* – a man of restless and versatile intellect – who, not content with an equivocal success in his own sphere of activity, plunges into scientific questions with which he has no real acquaintance, only to obscure them by an aimless rhetoric, and distract the attention of his hearers from the real point at issue by eloquent digressions and skilled appeals to religious prejudice.❞

This passage illustrates several techniques of speech-making, good and bad, but for the time being, simply savour the force Huxley put into the word 'rhetoric'. (Several people in the audience fainted at hearing a bishop so roughly handled.) It is an excellent example of a word being used as an emotional bullet for its audience, which is one of the oldest arts of speech-making. (What other words in the passage are doing the same job of making the audience boo at Wilberforce?)

After a century of abuse and decay, rhetoric is enjoying a revival, public speaking the way Aristotle taught it. It has started to reappear as a college course, particularly in the United States. More and more people are studying how to persuade others in speech, and even without the benefit of a formal course they are rediscovering the merits of Aristotle. There are still no better pillars for any speech than truth, pleasure and logic.

There are still no better pillars for any speech than truth, pleasure and logic.

No other medium has so much capacity to build *trust* as public speaking. Other media can certainly be pleasurable and sometimes even truthful and logical as well. But they do not have the same compulsion to be so, because they are more powerful and more versatile than the spoken word. They have more capacity to manufacture, manipulate and misinform. People are growing more aware of this: they are less willing to believe what they read in print, what they see and hear broadcast or on-line.

Compared to live speech, the output of other media is artificial – sometimes totally artificial. A newspaper article by a celebrity may be something he or she has never read, never mind written; a broadcast may be edited beyond recognition; an on-line identity may be completely invented.

Public speakers are not necessarily honest but they are real. They may be using words someone else has written, but at the moment of delivery they are out on their own. No one else can make them entertaining, persuasive or believable.

That is why Aristotle still works.

Words, words, words

Having decided to be truthful, entertaining and logical, a public speaker has only one basic means to achieve this.

If you want to speak well you need to know how to write.

There are different skills in speaking well, but ultimately a good speech depends on its words. The great speeches of history work on their own, on the printed page, without the aid of the orator's voice or the setting, the atmosphere or the audience response. If you want to speak well you need to know how to choose and organize words. In fact, you need to know how to write.

By writing well, you will go a long way to overcoming the errors and the terrors of public speaking and liberating the other skills which make a speech work.

The exhilaration of writing well will give you energy, unlock your imagination and allow you new insights about the most familiar and boring subject. There are few things that match the sensation of writing well. P. G. Wodehouse described it as a series of spasms. Tom Stoppard likened it to hitting a ball absolutely perfectly with a cricket bat. By writing well, your material will communicate your exhilaration to your audience. You will win their hearts and their minds (and votes and money) will follow.

The discipline of writing will make you think constantly and automatically about your objectives and how to organize your material to achieve them. The even tougher discipline of rewriting will sharpen you up even more, and take your words even quicker to their destination. When you have finished your (first) rewrite you will feel confident in your material, perhaps even eager to deliver it to its audience.

If you are speech-writing for somebody else, it is your job to transmit these gifts of exhilaration, tautness and confidence to another person, but you can still experience them vicariously. Your words are your children: you love them and are proud of them, even if someone else is taking care of them.

Speech-writing is a special craft but in some respects it is easier than other forms of writing.

For a start, it does not have to follow quite so many formal rules as written prose. In speech-writing, for example, it is perfectly all right to begin a sentence with 'And'. In fact, it is often a very effective device, which builds a bridge between thoughts for an audience. And in speech-writing you can often get away with verbless sentences. A single word can be a sentence. In a speech. Sometimes.

In speech-writing it is much easier to imagine the audience than in writing something to be read. You may know some or all of the audience personally. Even if you do not, you are much more likely to know what kind of people they are: you know who has invited them, you know the occasion and why they are likely to come (and whether they have eaten and drank). You also know the setting in which your words will be received. All of that information should help focus the content and style of your speech.

Compare writing a newspaper article. You may have a vague idea of the sort of people who read the newspaper, but it can never be too precise. Thousands of different people read any newspaper; they do not define themselves as an audience for you. There is no common purpose or setting between them and you. You do not know where and when, or even if, they will read your words. You have far less information about the audience of a newspaper article than that of a speech. (You would be wise to ignore this problem and concentrate on the audience-of-one: the editor who is going to pay for the newspaper article.)

Finally, speech-writing is a far more personal style of writing than written prose. A good speech is built on the personality of the speaker. When you understand that personality (whether it is your own or someone else's) your job as a speech-writer becomes very simple. You find the strengths of that personality and you set them free. You say 'I am (he is/she is) a scholar . . . a romantic . . . a joker . . . an idealist . . . a teacher . . . a motivator' and you write as a scholar, romantic, joker, idealist, teacher, motivator. When you have identified the personality who will be speaking, most of your work as a speech-writer is done. Of course you still have to do your research on the topic and the audience, you still have to organize your material, you will still have to weave in stories, jokes, fine images, sweeping passages and other 'big moments' and then cut most of them out of the final version (see the section in Chapter 10, 'All your little darlings must be killed').

But when you know the person who is speaking, all the other work is much easier.

Only you

No one else in the world can write or speak as well as you. You have a unique mind, a unique style, a unique command of your subject. You will discover this again in the section on overcoming nerves (see in Chapter 12, 'The man with egg on his suit').

But if you realize now that you are a wonderful speaker you will understand the purpose of this book. All the advice and the techniques and the analysis in this book are simply meant to help you discover what makes you so special. They have worked for other speakers, including the greatest in history. Read them and study them: they will certainly stop you making mistakes. But they will not *all* work for you. So pick and choose what does work for you. If you are getting laughs, tears, applause, when you want them by ignoring this book feel free to ignore it. Making speeches is not like playing bridge. It is not governed by rules and mathematics and systems. In speech-making there is no 'right' card to play.

No one else in the world can write or speak as well as you.

Having said that, I will now give you the one rule you may *not* ignore. *Be honest with yourself*. Read the section later on feedback. When you did it your way, when you broke all the rules, was it really a success? Did you really knock your audience dead? Or did you just hear what you wanted to hear?

You will find this very hard, and you will find it even harder if you are writing for someone else. First, because you may lose your job. Second, because you have someone else to blame. But you have no right to call yourself a speech-writer if you do not face up honestly to the response of your audience to your speech. If it did not really work, then try it my way.

The threefold noble truths

Three is a terrific number for speech-makers. I will suggest why later, but for now take it on trust and simply commit to memory the Three Noble Truths for all speeches:

1. Speak the Truth.
2. Listen for the Truth.
3. Be True to yourself.

You are now ready to make **High Impact Speeches**.

CHAPTER 1

Do I have to?

When to accept an invitation to speak

Before you even think about making a speech, ask yourself two big questions: *Do I have to do this?* and then *Do I want to do this?*

Strictly speaking, the answer to the first big question is usually No. You can certainly be a successful manager by paper and e-mail, or even chief officer of a leading organization. You can delegate all your speaking chores and cultivate a reputation for being deep and wise. The risk is that you may simply get a reputation for being dumb (and it is significant that dumb has come to mean not only silent but stupid). It could also make people think you arrogant or cowardly. Do you want that reputation, and can you afford to associate it with your business or your organization?

It is significant that dumb has come to mean not only silent but stupid.

So realistically, the answer to the first question will often be Yes. So refine the question. When you receive the invitation to speak, ask 'What will I/my organization lose if I do refuse? What will someone else gain by speaking in my place?'

That is a good way into another essential question: what would be my objectives in making this speech? Here are some likely answers:

- To win new customers for my product or service.
- To make people favour the interests of me and my organization or at least to stop them being hostile.
- To make people vote a certain way, or stop them voting a certain way.
- To promote a new product, new campaign, new idea.
- To be quoted in the media.

- To be recognized as the expert on an issue, the leading advocate of a cause.

And let us not forget:

- To show respect/give pleasure/boost motivation for whomever invited me.

Now you are ready to answer the second big question. Do I want to do this?

Run through that list of objectives again and write out the most negative response you can think of:

- These people will never be customers for my product or service (they are too poor, too resistant, too far away, too dependent on my competitor, etc.).
- *These people hate me and my organization and they always will.*
- These people always vote the wrong way, or not at all.
- *These people never listen to anything new.*
- Mr X is the authority on this and always will be.
- *I hate these people to bits and I do not care what they do or what happens to them.*

Notice how hard it is to justify all of these responses. 'Never' and 'always' are very strong statements. There is always a chance that you will change attitudes and behaviour (and market conditions) by giving a good speech. In fact the chance is good: if people ask you to speak to them, they have at least some interest in what you might say. Moreover, most people respect good manners, and a good speech is good manners. If you do no more than make people like you and respect you personally for your effort in speaking to them, your speech is probably worth doing.

Far more often than not, it is right to accept an invitation to speak – but only if you have the time and energy to prepare for it properly and do it single-mindedly. You should not speak at all unless it is the most important thing on your mind, indeed the only thing on your mind. That is the only way to give your speech energy and connect with your audience. People can tell instantly that you were not really interested in talking to them, and they will retaliate by not taking an interest in you. Bad manners makes a bad speech.

So, do not speak to anyone if your real motive is elsewhere. Suppose you are the CEO and your western branch invites you to speak at their annual dinner and dance. You would not normally give the speech (it only means you will have to do the same for the northern branch, and the east-

Bad manners makes a bad speech.

ern branch and the southern). But giving the speech will give you the chance to look over the underperforming western manager, and visit the new factory, and even see your daughter at western University . . .

In that case, don't give the speech. If the other things are that important, go West in your own time and attend to them. But don't you dare go through the motions at the dinner and dance. For your western employees it may well be the highlight of their working year. Show them respect. Give them a speech to match. If you won't do this, send someone who will.

There is one slight exception to this principle of single-minded attention to your audience. Very often you will want to talk to a wider audience than the live one in front of you. You will therefore be using your speech as a media opportunity, especially if you are campaigning for any cause. Some of your speech will be a press release or intended for broadcast news bulletins. Because of the size and reach of the media audience, these parts of your speech might take priority over those intended for the live audience. This

In politics the demands of the media can easily overwhelm the live audience.

might be reflected in the structure of your speech: the passages for broadcasting *must come early* so that they can be recorded and edited for the news bulletins. (This may also dictate when you want to appear in an order of speakers. If you are the star of the event, the organizers will want you to appear last. But if that means you miss the vital news bulletin or newspaper edition you may need to be ruthless and insist on appearing earlier.)

In politics the demands of the media can easily overwhelm the live audience. The cameras and the reporters plant themselves in the front row and jump up on the platform, so that the local people cannot see anything. The candidate delivers his or her media messages with gusto (sometimes more than once, because a camera jammed) and gabbles through the rest of the set speech. He or she puts in a few token references to the locality (cynical reporters tick off the references to the football team or the school band) and hurries away to the next place to repeat the formula.

Even in politics there is no excuse for speaking like that. It makes local audiences despise you. It does not even work for the media: do you want them to report a cold reception? For all the demands of the media you should still make your live audience feel that they are all important. Of course you will craft your speech for the media, but you can and should also wow the people in front of you (and win television images of a wildly cheering crowd). The master of this was Bill Clinton. I covered his first presidential election campaign, when he sometimes delivered 20 speeches on the same day. Even in the 20th speech he still made everyone in his live audience feel that he was talking to him or her as an individual.

If you cannot be Bill Clinton, do not give a live speech.

If you cannot be Bill Clinton, do not give a live speech. Do all your campaigning from a studio.

Speech-making opportunities to avoid

Apart from this general principle of being completely focused on your speech, there are some specific circumstances in which it is usually wiser to decline the invitation to speak.

One is when you are certain that the event has been organized by 'the enemy'. If you represent a tobacco company, there is not much point in addressing the Anti-Smoking League. In general, it is not worth defending hunting to an audience of animal lovers. Meetings of highly partisan organizations tend to be filled with its committed supporters, people whose minds are made up. They come to its meetings to confirm their opinions (some will come specifically to ambush you, to try to make you angry or look silly and the person in charge of the meeting may well let them get away with it).

Although you will win some marks for good manners by turning up at the enemy meeting, and although your speech will of course be brilliant and powerful, you will almost certainly fail to overcome the prejudice of a self-selecting audience.

When you want to reach out to your enemy, find a chance to do it in a neutral forum (like a civic organization or a charity) with a neutral person in the chair.

Conversely, consider carefully before you speak to a meeting of your own most partisan supporters, including employees. It is a waste of energy confirming their own prejudices. In fact, by attracting them to a meeting you are actually preventing them from talking to uncommitted people – potential voters in politics, potential customers in business. Talk to your own people only if you need to boost their morale or induce them to make some fresh effort, or when you want them to hear and promote a new message.

Politicians frequently talk to their own supporters to get a cheering backdrop for television cameras and to ensure a supply of soft questions. I think this is a mistake on two counts. First, party supporters resent being treated as extras on a movie set. Second, all such meetings look synthetic and phoney to the media and the outside world. Don't follow the politicians. Speak to your own supporters when you really have something to say to them. Show them respect.

Organizations on the fringe of politics are often totally unscrupulous.

You should also consider whether you want your name and your organization's to be associated with the people inviting you. They may be extremists, or in some way offensive to other important audiences whom you have to reach. Moreover, in my experience, organizations on the fringe of politics are often totally unscrupulous. If you speak to them they identify you ever after as a supporter, and continue to do so no matter how often you correct this. They may take your picture in apparent agreement or friendship with their leaders and circulate it.

If you think you might be set up in this way, do *not* accept an invitation to speak. One useful tip: extremist organizations of Right or Left often conceal themselves under high-sounding names. Those of the Right often like to use the word Freedom and those of the Left will claim to be defending cherished rights. (Apologies to all the organizations which genuinely support freedom and cherished rights, but they will know what liberties are taken with their names.)

If you, or your boss, get invited to speak by a strange, high-sounding organization, research it very thoroughly. Visit its website. Get copies of its publications. Ask for its articles of association and its officers. Check out its donors. Find out who has spoken at any of its previous meetings. Find press reports of those meetings, and do not rely on the organization's own account. If any of these things produce a health warning about the organization, stay away from it.

I would also recommend staying well away from any fringe religious congregation.

Finally, you should blacklist any organization which double-crossed you in the past. If you were induced to speak by promises which were not kept, or if you were ambushed at a meeting by a sudden change of rules, or unplanned speakers or events – do not speak to that organization again. Do not let them get away with that kind of behaviour. Let them know why you have struck them off. You owe that not just to yourself but to other speakers. If the organization was merely incompetent rather than discourteous (for example, they failed to publicize your last meeting), you might give them a second chance, but make it very clear in your acceptance what they must do to make amends. Other speech-making opportunities to avoid:

Mass open air rallies

Unless you are a superb stump speaker, these are not good occasions to put over a message. The audience will be too noisy and too excitable and likely to shout. It may well be infiltrated by fringe groups from its own side of the political spectrum, and attract protestors from the other. As a speaker you will be at the mercy of the weather and the sound amplification system, and possibly even the police.

Badly structured debates

There are a number of well-recognized forms for debates. If you are invited to a debate which does not follow any of these forms, you should probably avoid it. Be especially wary of 'debates' where you are to be sandwiched between many other speakers, which have no set proposition for people to vote for and against, and those which offer the prospect of lengthy contributions from the floor.

Too many other speakers

I would never want to share a meeting with more than three other platform speakers (except for certain structured debates, which might have three speakers on each side).

Audience is too foreign

Be very cautious before speaking to an audience where no one, or very few people, can understand you. In those circumstances you will need complete faith in your interpreter(s). Remember that there will probably be informal interpreters at such a meeting – people who think they understand something you have said and decide to explain it or comment on it to their neighbours. With a very foreign audience, you need to be certain that what you say is what they hear.

With a foreign audience you will also need to be fully briefed on their social habits and their wider culture, for example, their dress codes, their speaking conventions, their interpretations of gestures and body language. If you are not confident of mastering all these details, do not take the risk of speaking to them. A prime purpose of giving a speech is to show respect to an audience: you will undo this completely if you unconsciously insult them.

A speech is unnecessary

It is curious how often people invite a speaker to events where he or she simply is not needed, and gets in the way of the real purpose. Perhaps they think that a speech adds dignity to the occasion: in fact it simply adds boredom and irritation. When people go to a dog show, they do not need a speech, however fascinating. They just want to see the dogs. Don't delay them. If you like dogs, or want to reach the dog-loving audience, accept the invitation but don't give a set speech. Declare the event open in one sentence and shake hands with the people and the dogs.

SUMMARY

- In general, it pays to accept an invitation to speak rather than refuse it.

- But before accepting, you must be ready to give the speech your full energy and not be distracted by other tasks and priorities.

- Don't let media demands take over completely from the needs of your live audience.

- Refuse any invitation from any organization which cheated on you in the past.

- Avoid speaking to very partisan, hostile audiences.

- Consider carefully your purpose in speaking to very partisan, friendly audiences.

- Don't talk to any organization if you do not want to be associated with it and its supporters.

- Think very carefully before talking to
  - mass open air rallies
  - unstructured debates
  - meetings with too many speakers
  - very foreign audiences
  - the dog show.

What you must research

Your essential subjects: the venue and the audience

Having accepted the invitation to speak at Snodsbury Civic Forum, you must now do your essential research.

Answer the most important question first: what is the last train home from Snodsbury? (Or when are the flights out from Snodsbury Airport?)

It is never worth driving yourself to a speaking engagement. You do not need the extra stress of driving, and there is too much risk that you will rehearse your speech at the wheel and lose concentration. The police and the courts will not accept a defence of driving while intoxicated with your own oratory. When you are tired, angry and already late you do not need the stress of trying to read the map which your hosts have sent. It will bear no relationship to the Snodsbury through which you are trying to navigate: none of the landmarks on the map will appear, and the host's chosen route will make no allowance for the new one-way system. Finally, you will discover that the 'Snodsbury Hall' to which you were invited has been renamed the Sylvain Legwinski Auditorium and signposted accordingly.

Sort out the practical issues first.

It is equally stressful to be driven to a speaking engagement if your chauffeur is lost. (If you are that chauffeur – be honest. Do not pretend that you know what you are doing and that the Hall is five minutes away. Pull into the nearest recognizable place where you can park and tell your speaker what has happened. Phone your host and tell him what has happened. Do not rely on any further instructions from him, or any local person. Call a taxi instead.)

I am saying: sort out the practical issues first. Establish the time and the place of the speaking engagement in your diary and in your mind. Establish the format of the event. When exactly will you be speaking? Whom will you follow or precede? How much time will you have? When can you politely get away? Are you expected to do anything else (answer questions, declare something open, present an award, draw raffle tickets)? When do you eat? Will the audience have eaten? What is the venue like? How many does it hold? Will it be full? What technical equipment will you be able to use?

Do not even think about the speech until you have thoroughly researched *the audience*.

Rid yourself (or your boss) of all the basic worries about any engagement. You are now free to start composing the speech . . .

Wrong. Absolutely wrong. Do not even think about the speech until you have thoroughly researched *the audience*.

Your task is much easier if the audience is by invitation only rather than open to all. However, in either case you should try to establish:

- the likely age range of the audience and any concentrations of age groups (especially of very old or very young)
- the likely gender balance
- the likely faith groups
- the likely ethnic mix (how many will not have English as first language?)
- will any have hearing difficulties?

The organizer of the event should be able to give you this kind of basic information (especially on the last point: it is his or her job, not yours, to meet any special physical needs of audience members). All of it has a bearing on the content, length and organization of your speech. It can stop you boring, mystifying or offending major parts of your audience.

For example, with an audience of children you will choose a subject which is accessible to them and talk about it in a plain style, using simple language. But you will not talk down to them, something which children despise, and in particular you will not try to use any of their special slang.

Children have a particularly strong sense of logic and sequence, so you will take particular care with these aspects of your speech. If you are presenting an argument to children, you will spell out very clearly your supporting reasons (it helps to use the word 'because' as often as possible). If you are telling them a story, you will tell it in the right narrative order.

You might want to grab their attention with a particularly striking visual aid or display. But an even better attention device is to get children to participate in your speech. Build in moments for them to answer questions or at least put up their hands.

Needless to say, with children you will cut out any jokes which might seem off-colour. Needless to say? Unfortunately not. I once heard a TV comedian produce his cheesy nightclub act in a primary school. He was not asked back.

These are important points about speaking to children. They are not rocket science, but common sense. I spelt them out to show the simple benefits of thinking about your audience. The same common-sense thinking will produce equally vital guides to speaking to other broad categories of people. For example, with teenagers and young adults: act your age, not theirs. For older people: don't be patronizing. Older audiences tend to be smarter than younger ones, and they nearly always know a great deal more.

For older people: don't be patronizing.

Appeal to their experience and wisdom. For faith groups and minority ethnic audiences: don't pretend to be one of them if you are not, but take special care not to use excluding language or arguments or offensive or patronizing references. For people who have hearing problems or are not especially fluent in English: speak more carefully than usual (so reduce the normal content of your speech) and don't rely on highly 'literary' effects.

For any audience with women: don't use male-only language (you can avoid it) and don't tell jokes which patronize or offend women.

If women are an especially important part of the audience, you should remember that women are generally more imaginative than men. They have the ability to recognize more arguments and possible positions on any issue. If you are trying to persuade a largely female audience you should therefore try to avoid strongly *reductionist* arguments, the ones that say: 'You do not support Position A, that means you must support Position B.'

This kind of information is essential for planning your speech. You get it from very basic, common-sense thinking about your audience.

Now analyze your audience more deeply. What common factor will bring them all to the venue (apart from your brilliance as a speaker)? Are they all members of an organization? Are they linked by occupation, faith, common interest or common cause?

Now analyze your audience more deeply.

This analysis will guide your choice of topic (if you have any choice) and your approach to it. Suppose you are talking to the National Association of Beekeepers. Good topics would include 'What Bees Can Teach Business', 'Great Bees in History', 'Bee Disease and How to Avoid It' or even, 'Why I Hate Bees'. If you know nothing about bees but a great deal about taxation, you could and should build a bridge to your audience with 'The Tax Threat to Bees'. Whatever you are talking about, you will use the world of bees for your analogies and supporting arguments. You would relate any numbers you use to numbers of bees, as in 'That cost the taxpayer £x million – the equivalent of £10 for every bee in Britain'.

Identifying your audience will not always be this easy. You may have nothing to go on except the *place* you have been invited to. Take my opening example: Snodsbury Civic Forum. The only thing you know about this audience is that they are concerned citizens of Snodsbury. In that case, study Snodsbury. Of course you will ask the organizer about the place and what kind of people go to the Civic Forum. But do your own research as well. Find out everything possible about the locality, its history, its economic and social life, its customs and current concerns. (Hint: if you want an instant political and social snapshot of anywhere in the USA or the UK, look it up in the *Almanac of American Politics*, or its counterpart the *Almanac of British Politics*.)

If your audience is locally defined, do this exercise. Read the local paper and use your imagination to link your subject to the headline story. You want to talk about energy conservation, the *Snodsbury Echo* leads with the threat to the local bus service. You might open your remarks by thinking about all the extra car journeys which would happen in Snodsbury without the bus – all guzzling gas. That was not difficult was it? There might not be a link to the headline story, but somewhere in the local paper there will be something which you can use to illustrate your big topic and break it down into something relevant for your audience. It might be the school history pageant (how did local people get to the pageant 100 years ago? How much energy did they use?). Or even an advertisement – the summer special offer on air conditioners.

However your audience is defined, keep asking yourself these questions:

- Who are these people?
- What would they want to hear about?
- What frame of reference should I use to punch home my points?
- What kind of jokes will they appreciate?

Now try to imagine whether the audience really wants to come out to your speaking event or whether they will be coming reluctantly, because they feel they have to. In the first category might be the annual dinner dance of the local amateur football club. People choose to join the football club, they choose to pay for tickets to its dinner dance. Barring a few who have been pushed into it by their partners and families, they want to be there.

In the second category might be a farmers' protest meeting. Most farmers work long hours right through the year. They have nearly always got better things to do than go to any meeting. This is even more true for poor people. Think for a minute about the barriers which might stop poor people coming to hear you speak. Arranging child care . . . no personal transport . . . fear of crime returning home at night . . . need to use time to work or learn – or sleep.

You need to work harder on your speech for a reluctant audience.

Quite simply, you need to work harder on your speech for a reluctant audience. Choose a topic which is totally relevant to them (How Business Can Help Farmers . . . Increase Child Benefit Now . . . Save Public Transport). Make all your imagery and references totally accessible to them. It is like talking to the beekeepers, only more so. With a reluctant audience you must be ready to annihilate yourself. Keep completely focused on their needs and interests. Show that you appreciate the sacrifice that they have made by coming to hear you.

If the audience is not only reluctant but potentially hostile, you will need to be more than relevant, you will need to build an alliance. Be prepared to take a lot of time saying things that (most of) the audience will agree with before you bring them to your desired conclusion (we will discuss this further in Chapter 9). With a potentially hostile audience you will have to be a lion tamer – don't turn your back on them for a second. In speech-making terms, turning your back on an audience means any sequence whose purpose is clear to you but not transparently clear to them.

With a potentially hostile audience you will have to be a lion tamer – don't turn your back on them for a second.

With a friendly or neutral audience you can use such sequences deliberately and very effectively. For example, you might well spend a minute, or even longer, setting out an opposing point of view in order to knock it down in one sentence. You cannot do this with a potentially hostile audience. A minute, even a second, is too long to leave them in suspense. Do not use any sequence, any literary technique, which can misdirect them. Do not even use basic irony (the kind where you say something and then say 'Not . . .' or 'Yeah, right . . .'). It is just too dangerous. Be direct throughout your speech.

You simply cannot do too much research and analysis of your audience. A High Impact Speech is not only well-crafted, well-written, well-delivered, but builds a personal bridge between the speaker and the audience. Bill Clinton could do this naturally. The rest of us have to work on it.

SUMMARY

- When you accept a speaking engagement, begin by mastering all the practical details, especially how to get there and back.
- Then thoroughly research your audience.
- Check the likely age, gender, ethnic, faith profile of your audience (and whether there will be people with hearing difficulties) and be prepared to adjust your speech and style accordingly.
- Identify the special common factor which unites your audience and choose your subject and your supporting material accordingly.
- Make your speech locally relevant.
- Identify your audience as willing, reluctant or potentially hostile. Be especially relevant for the reluctant. For the potentially hostile, build alliances and always speak directly not obliquely.

I came here for a result

Planning the right impact

You have now done a lot of essential work – deciding whether to speak at all, finding out how to get there and what you have to do, and *researching the audience thoroughly*. The rest of your speech will be easier and easier.

Are you ready to start writing? Not quite. There is one further essential step. Decide what you want your speech to achieve. We have touched on this already, but now it is time to do a specific exercise.

Decide what you want your speech to achieve.

Take a piece of paper, a black pen and a red pen. With the black pen you will now write down (1), (2) and (3). Against these also in black pen, you will write down the general aims of your speech. Why three? Because three is the magic number in speech-making.

Now take the red pen and write alongside each aim any specific actions you want the audience to do at the end of your speech. Here are some sample exercises.

* *

Speech One: The Story of Felix the Cat

Black pen   Red pen

Aims   Audience action

1. Inform audience of history and   Buy my Felix book
   cultural significance of cartoon
   character Felix the Cat
2. Persuade audience Felix was greatest   Join Felix Society
   cartoon character ever

3. Delight/impress audience	Ecstactic applause Flood of new invitations to speak

Speech Two: Retirement of Mr X, long-serving employee

Black pen	Red pen
Aims	Audience action
1. Remind/inform audience of Mr X's career, achievements, character	Mr X accepts offer of part-time consultancy
2. Thank contributors to retirement fund, remind latecomers fund still open	More contributions
3. Show organization values employees	Discontented employees A, B, C seek private conversation about grievances

Speech Three: Debate speech for/against joining the euro

Black pen	Red pen
Aims	Audience action
1. Persuade audience to be for/against euro	Vote for/against euro
2. Make audience remember (up to) three key facts/arguments	Pick up handout with key facts
3. Make audience realize importance of euro to their business, community, family, personal lives	Give money Join euro organization Write to MP

This exercise is vital for any **High Impact Speech.** By definition a high impact speech is one which meets its objectives: if you do not know your objectives you cannot make any impact.

Three quick points before we leave the exercise. First, you may not always come up with three aims for every speech, but it is helpful to try. If you are really stuck for anything to write against (2) or (3) you can always put: Make Them Love Me.

Second, you will not always have a red-ink entry against each of the black-ink aims. For example, in Speech Two, perhaps you do not want Mr X to come back, and perhaps there are no malcontented employees to talk to privately. In these circumstances, the red-ink section might have been blank. Once again, it is helpful to think of something to put in the red-ink section (you can always fall back on Ecstatic Applause).

Third, and most important, you may not always be able to achieve all of your desired aims and audience outcomes.

This is particularly true of the debate speech. You may not have the time or the opportunity to induce the audience to do anything more than vote the way you want to. In an organized debate it is often bad manners to ask for money or signatures or to hand out anything, and many organizers will actually prohibit these things from any speaker. As to the aims, you may only have enough speaking time to win the debate. That is your short-term aim, and your job as part of the team. You cannot waste time on longer-term objectives and again it might be bad manners to do so. Debating is a team effort and you have no right to 'annex' the audience for any personal objectives without agreement from the rest of the team.

Even if you are the lone speaker you may have to reject one aim or intended audience response because it militates against another. In Speech Two, for example, aim 3 (about your organization) may get in the way of aim 1 (about Mr X). If so, you will have to sacrifice it, because if you do not achieve aim 1 (appreciating the long-serving employee) you are not going to achieve aim 3 anyway (making all employees feel appreciated).

Even if you do have to downplay or sacrifice one aim of your speech, it will still be immensely valuable to have written it down. It will force you to think about priorities and structure.

You have now identified your audience and your aims. You are almost ready to write the first line of your speech: the title.

Before that, pause a little longer and review your aims. You will probably find that they fall into one of three broad headings: to inform your audience about something, to arouse their emotions about something (including yourself), or to persuade them to accept a point of view and possibly to do something in consequence. Some books on speeches formally divide them on those lines, and suggest different approaches for informative, or emotional, or persuasive speeches.

Review your aims.

It is a mistake to make these categories too rigid, because you must do a little of all three jobs in any speech. You cannot persuade people without giving them reliable information and engaging their emotions. If you want people to accept information, you must persuade them of its value to them. That judgement depends on a point of view: this information deserves to be understood and remembered.

Finally, you cannot simply play on an audience's emotions. This may seem surprising. Many famous and infamous speeches seem to be built on nothing but emotion. But emotion presupposes a point of view. People do not simply laugh and cry, they do so because it is right for them to laugh and cry. To make it right for them to laugh or cry, they need information to support that point of view. Even a speech which is meant to be pure entertainment needs a bedrock of facts and values. It cannot simply be a string of jokes and one-liners. Analyze any worthwhile comedian and you will find that his or her material is always built on a logical sequence, or a series of logical self-contained sequences. Each sequence will invariably contain enough facts to let the audience understand the comedian's context and embody an attitude to the subject which the audience must share. The most off-the-wall comedian has to inform and persuade to get laughs.

Take some trouble to choose an accurate title.

All that being said, your statement of aims will probably put your speech into one of the three primary categories: informing, persuading, emotional. If you have any choice in the matter, the title of your speech should reflect this. It is your first shot at achieving your aims and it works for you before you even see the audience. So take some trouble to choose an accurate title.

If your primary purpose is *information*, keep your title factual and free of loaded words. For example, 'The Oil Industry Today'.

If you want to *persuade*, signal your point of view in the title. For example, 'The Oil Industry: Saving the World from Poverty'.

If you want people to feel *emotion*, load it into the title, preferably in front of the subject. Perhaps 'The Friend in your Home – The Oil Industry' or 'The Lonely Genius of the Oil Industry'. (I have to say that protesters against the oil industry have an easier time with emotional titles.)

The last example illustrates another point about titles. Some are 'open', some are 'closed'. An open title leaves the speaker free to deal with the topic as he or she pleases. A closed one channels the topic and defines at least some of the information which will go into it. The choice is yours. The advantage of a closed topic is obviously that you do not have to talk – or answer questions from the audience – about anything outside it. You may even legitimately close the topic right down to a very narrow segment. 'The Lonely Genius of the Oil Industry' will be an admiring profile of one brilliant prospector, or inventor or engineer or business leader (if you compose this speech think who would play your subject in the movie). You may open up this topic by suggesting that such individual genius is typical of the industry, but you do not have to.

The open topic ('Saving the World from Poverty') allows you to be more selective and individual in your approach, but it exposes you to a wider range of questions from the audience. Even without direct questions you will have to justify to the audience your approach to the topic and deal with the arguments against it (more on this in Chapter 9). In other words, you may have to do more work.

Whatever title you select, the golden rule is to let your audience know what to expect and then stick to it. If you choose 'The Oil Industry', do not disappoint your audience of business students by a long propaganda tract. Conversely, if you choose 'Saving the World from Poverty' do not give a dry economics lecture. Keep faith with your audience (especially if they are reluctant or potentially hostile).

Very frequently, your speech will not have a title at all, especially when you are speaking at a special occasion. Here, it is worth keeping in mind the distinction between open and closed topics. Some occasions are more or less 'open', and you can handle them more or less as you please. An example is being guest speaker at a school prizegiving. You must of course thank the school and praise it, but otherwise you may select any topic which is relevant and appropriate to a school audience. Other occasions are 'closed'. A funeral tribute must be about the deceased and it is poor taste to talk about anything else (although Shakespeare's Mark Anthony got away with it).

On other occasions you may have a title which you did not choose. An obvious example is when you take part in a debate. Your effective title is being for or against the proposition. Another example might be testifying in court, or before any committee of inquiry. Still another might be accepting an invitation to deliver the annual memorial lecture to a learned society. The people who endow such lectures often control the title from beyond the grave.

Even if you have no title for your speech, or are stuck with someone else's, it is worth composing an ideal title for yourself. This exercise gives a useful check on the aims of your speech, and it will also set your mind thinking productively about its structure and content. The ideal title should fit the statement of aims and intended responses which you wrote earlier in the black and red ink. It should also of course be compatible with the occasion and/or the title handed down to you.

You have now identified your audience and your objectives and thought up a perfect title for your speech, either one which will actually be used or an imaginary one to help you focus. Can we now start writing the speech? Not quite. Go back to that perfect title and tinker with it. Even small changes will stimulate your mind and make you identify what you really want to talk about.

One very productive method of tinkering is to add different prepositions to your ideal title. Another is to change the tenses of any verbs in your title, real or implied. Suppose you have hit on 'Felix the Cat: The Greatest Cartoon Character in History'. Try rewriting this in succession as 'When/Where/How/Why Felix the Cat [Became/Is] the Greatest Cartoon Character in History'.

Each of these gives you a different speech. Each one is persuasive, in that you will be trying to make the audience agree with your point of view about Felix. But the supporting structure will be different. When . . . will be built on the history of cartoons. Where . . . might talk about the movie theatre where Felix was first shown (and the riot he caused). How . . . would analyze the plots, the artwork, the innovatory animation techniques which went into Felix. Why . . . would compare Felix to all possible rivals. One of these is your speech.

SUMMARY

- Write a plan of at most three basic aims for your speech in black ink and then in red ink, what you intend the audience to do.
- Try to fill out this plan even if you know you must limit your objectives.
- Think about the primary purpose of your speech – information, persuasion or emotion – even though every speech must contain something of all three.
- Choose a title that matches your primary purpose and which is honest with your audience.
- Think about whether your speech topic or occasion is 'open' or 'closed' and how much freedom you have to choose your content.
- Compose an ideal title for your speech even if you know you cannot use it.
- Play around with your chosen title.

CHAPTER 4

Speech architecture

Planning the right structure

Having at last completed your audience research, worked out the aims and intended results and equipped yourself with a title, you can now start to write it.

Wrong. You would not start building a house without a plan and you do not build a speech without an architect's design. Invest time and effort in that design and it will be repaid handsomely. Your speech will be built much quicker and it will not fall down.

All speeches have essentially the same architecture.

Unlike houses, all speeches have essentially the same architecture. There is an Introduction, a Beginning, a Middle and an End. Moreover, they tend to come in standard sizes. If the speech itself is the standard size of 20 minutes, the Introduction will (generally) be 1–2 minutes the Beginning another 2 minutes, the Middle 13–15 minutes and the End 2 minutes. The Introduction, the Beginning and the End need at least that amount of time, and if you can invest more in them it will repay you to do so. So if you have 40 minutes to speak, do not throw all the extra 20 minutes into the Middle. Divide at least 10 of the extra minutes between the Introduction, the Beginning and the End.

The Introduction

Speech-makers are often given this advice: start by telling them what you are going to say, say it, and finish by telling them what you have said.

That is perfectly good advice – but only if you remember to give yourself an introduction before the beginning of your speech.

A separate introduction serves many purposes. The first is good manners. You use the introduction to thank anyone you must thank, your introducer, the organizers of the event, the singer(s)/orchestra/actors who performed so brilliantly, the child who presented the bouquet. Thank everybody, even if it makes your speech sound like an Oscar winner.

The first thing you must write down in your speech plan is:

> Introduction
> Thank yous

The second purpose of your introduction is to allow your audience to settle down. Even if you are speaking well down the programme, there may be some latecomers trying to shuffle into their places under cover of the stormy applause for the host introducing you. Even without them, it is an iron law of public speaking that each new speaker on the platform attracts a new cougher in the audience.

The third and most important purpose is to connect. Your introduction makes you part of the event and builds an essential bridge between you and the audience. It should make them like you and respect you *before* you try to tell them anything important. Your speech plan should now read:

> Introduction
> Thank yous
> Connect

The copious audience research you have done might suggest some ways of connecting instantly with your audience. In your next indent, under *Connect* you might jot down some of the material you have uncovered, for example, the local headline story, and a way of incorporating it into your introduction. One possibility might be the bus service under threat of cancellation:

> Bus 37 — promise to finish before last bus (may not be another for 10 years)

However, there is a risk in getting too close to your audience too quickly. If you are a stranger, there is no reason for you to know or care about Bus 37. People might think it presumptuous of you to mention it, almost like gatecrashing their community. It is also a trick which is associated with politicians. Save Bus 37 for a little later, when they trust you.

Instead, there is one absolutely reliable way to connect with any audience, and your plan should now read:

```
Introduction
  Thank yous
  Connect
● praise host organization
● praise locality
● praise setting
```

If there is nothing local about your audience you will of course drop the reference to locality. If the setting is totally boring and functional, and reflects no glory back on the host organization, drop that reference too. But there is nearly always something interesting about any setting which will make it worth mentioning. The great 'connective' merit of the host organization and the setting is that these are common frames of reference for you and your audience. By complimenting them, you compliment your audience automatically (we should be proud to be in such a fine place, associated with such a fine organization).

Here is a plan for the introduction of a speech to the National Bee Association in Snodsbury:

```
Introduction
  Thank yous
  Connect
● praise host orgn (grown from 1,000 members 1920 to
  1m+, now largest bee orgn in world)
● praise Snodsbury, if Mayor there (home of the
  legendary Snodsbury Sound in rock-n-roll history)
● praise hall (award-winning acoustics — can you
  hear me at back?)
```

By doing such a plan in this way, you will make your introduction very easy to write. You may also stimulate good thoughts or good jokes, so capture them right away.

If you are very clever you might be able to connect with the audience and deliver a key message at the same time. You might praise the organization, or locality, or setting within the special context of your speech. One successful example took place at a lecture by Mr Vernon Ellis, the International Chairman of Accenture, under the title 'Enterprise or Exploitation: Can Global Business Be a Force for Good?'

This was a 'big', abstract subject: the lecture's main body covered a lot of ground and had a 'big', thoughtful message to convey. To make matters harder for the speaker, he had a very disparate audience to reach.

Mr Ellis had yet another potential problem. He was speaking in one of London's finest buildings – the Banqueting Hall created by Inigo Jones with a famous ceiling by Rubens. Many of his audience were visiting for the first time, and were gawping in admiration.

He turned their wonderment to his own advantage – using the setting to deliver some key messages. He said:

  "It is a special pleasure to be here in the magnificent surroundings of the Banqueting House, the revolutionary masterpiece of Inigo Jones.

Of course, Inigo Jones was a businessman as well as an architect, and one who benefited from global markets and the opening of trade. By travelling to Italy he learnt not only to be a classical architect but a stage designer who brought England the proscenium arch and moveable scenery. Like so many artists throughout history, Inigo Jones illustrates the benefits of free movement across frontiers.

There is another lesson for business leaders in this marvellous setting – a lesson in the perils of ignoring the society around them. It was from a window in this Banqueting House that King Charles the First walked to the scaffold. Now when Charles ruled without Parliament he financed his government (and this wonderful Rubens ceiling) by giving monopolies in essential products to his business supporters. The monopolies were extremely unpopular. His subjects boycotted the Royal products and the King ran out of money. He had to recall Parliament and the English civil war was set in motion. The monopo-

lies were bad politics which became bad business, and they exposed Charles to the ultimate form of hostile takeover. "

In this passage, the speaker flattered his audience for being there, and for their knowledge of history, and conveyed vividly two complex ideas, the benefits of open markets and the peril of divorcing business from the concerns of wider society. He also made a good, relevant joke. Nice work.

For the rest of this chapter we are going to study the Beginning, the Middle and the End by planning one imaginary speech. The planning lessons will be relevant for any speech, although a speech to be used in debate has some special needs which we will look at separately.

The imaginary speech is the annual lecture to a community college in a middle-sized town in the American Mid West. The title, by the speaker's choice is 'President Harry Truman: Creator of the Modern World'. (Don't worry if you know nothing about Truman – everything will make sense. For the time being, remember that he was President of the United States from 1945 to 1953.)

This is primarily a speech to inform but it must also persuade the audience of a possibly controversial point of view. (Truman left office 50 years ago – why is he even relevant to modern world, let alone its creator?) And with 40 minutes to fill on a hot summer day the speaker had better produce some emotion and engagement from the audience. In terms of 'open' or 'closed', we might call it a 'semi-open' topic: the speaker must stick to Truman, but has some latitude over the aspects of Truman to be included.

Because I am getting tired of saying 'the speaker' and would like to use pronouns easily, this particular speaker is a woman. First, watch her plan the Introduction:

```
Introduction
  Thank you (host recently honoured by Am Hist Assn)
  Connect
  • praise college (famous alumni, record baseball
    season — all in prospectus)
  • praise town (record of volunteering in war and
    peace — people who take responsibility like
    Truman) R? did Truman stop here 1948 election
```

As in the previous example, by complimenting the audience in the context of the main subject, she will be able to give a sneak preview of part of the main message.

The symbol R? with underlining is a good way to flag up essential points to be *researched*, questions whose answer will have an important influence on the speech. Very frequently, you will use this symbol to seek out the 'killer fact' (see Chapter 9). Now we will proceed to the Beginning.

The Beginning

Having displayed your good manners and successfully connected yourself to the event and the audience, you have earned the right to claim their full attention. This is the moment to do it. You may lose them later, so now is the time to play what Americans call a 'grabber' – something arresting, compelling, dramatic which at the same time supports your key message and sets up your main themes. So in the plan write down now:

```
Beginning
   Grabber
   Main themes
```

The grabber can be almost anything – a joke, an anecdote, a quotation, a fantasy, a visual aid, a hyperbole, a startling fact or statement. This is where you might well exploit your local knowledge – after they have accepted you. To make it work, you should be able to deliver it without reading anything.

If your speech is topical and the media are present, you may have to tailor the grabber to their needs, rather than the live audience. Print journalists need a headline and the first two paragraphs of a story. Broadcast journalists need a clip which they can use in a news bulletin. Both categories are almost certainly working to deadlines: do not keep them waiting for the 'story' in your speech. If you do, it may not be reported. If the media are going to be present, use as your grabber the one sentence which you want to be remembered from your speech. It may mean using something you would far prefer to place elsewhere. If Lincoln had been televised at Gettysburg his media advisers would have made him *open* with 'Fellow countrymen, we highly resolve that government of the people, by the people, for the people shall not perish from the earth', rather than leaving it until the end.

In any circumstances, a grabber should normally be short, and remember particularly that if your grabber is a visual aid it needs to disappear when it has done its job. If you leave it with the audience it grabs attention *away* from you.

In our Truman example, the speaker has got an each-way bet on her grabber. Her research might providentially reveal that Truman spoke at the host town in his famous whistle-stop election tour in 1948. If so, she might quote contemporary news reports of his visit and the response he got. This would be a very effective, sustained grabber, especially if the reports mentioned local people who are still alive or still have families in the town.

Failing an actual visit, a different piece of research could produce a different, much shorter grabber. Did the town vote for Truman in 1948? Then the speaker might say: 'In 1948, this town changed the world for ever. It voted for Harry Truman in the presidential election.'

If the research shows that the town voted against Truman, she could spin this information around to produce another short grabber. She might say something like: 'Harry Truman loved this town, even though it did not vote for him. He loved all towns like this. He was born in one and grew up in it and went back to live there when he left the Presidency. He once called towns like this the "strong centre of America". He did an immense amount for this town. In fact he changed its life for ever, along with America's and the world's.'

Any one of these three beginnings should flatter the audience and make them sit up. So here is what they might look like in the plan:

```
Beginning
  Grabber
    1. R? Truman here in 1948. Reports. R? Local names
       in reports OR
    2. R? Truman wins here in 1948. Town changed history
       OR
    3. R? Truman loses here in 1948. T loved town
       anyway, loved all towns like it, small town
       himself, changed town for ever + US + world
```

I mentioned that debates are different. If you are replying to another speaker you should not completely ignore what he or she said. The opposition may have made some headway with the audience – eliminate this before you ask for their full attention. Separate this demolition job from the grabber. You do not want people to think about the opposition when you go for your big moment.

As number 2 or below in a debate, the plan for your beginning should therefore look like this:

```
The Beginning
  Demolish opposition
  Grabber
  Main themes
```

Having grabbed their attention, you will now tell your audience what you are going to tell them. This is where you will set out, as simply as possible, the main themes of the speech.

Try to hit the magic speech-making number of three. If you have more than three themes, collapse them into three. There is always some way of doing this. For example, a recent survey of American business executives[1] identified six distinct styles of business leadership: 'coercive' (do what I tell you); 'pacesetting' (do as I do, now); 'coaching' (try this); 'democratic' (what do you think?); 'affiliative' (how do you feel?); 'authoritative' (let's do this together). Suppose you want to make a speech about them. If you stick to these six as major themes you may find yourself running out of time and there is a good chance that some will not lodge in your audience's mind. But without too much effort you could organize them in three groups of two. You might achieve this with three colourful, and memorably alliterative, images. Coercive and pacesetting might go together under the heading of The Platoon Sergeant, democratic and affiliative might be grouped under The Politician, coaching and authoritative could be The Parent.

In the Truman speech example, the speaker has no difficulty organizing three main themes. Here's how they look on her plan:

---

[1] 'Leadership that gets results', Daniel Goleman, Harvard Business Review' March–April 2000. Presented and analysed in *Working With Americans* by Allyson Stewart-Allen and Lanie Deneslow (Prentice Hall Business, 2002), Chapter 6.

```
The Beginning
  Grabber (1) OR (2) OR (3)
  Main themes
  1. How Truman changed the USA R? impact on town
  2. How Truman changed the world
  3. The Truman model of leadership.
```

These main themes are definite choices. They will not be changed. Although she has flagged up the need to research what Truman did for the host town, the result will illustrate theme 1, not replace it with anything else.

These were by no means the only possible choices as main themes. She might have approached the subject chronologically, say (1) Truman as care-taker 1945–1949; (2) President in own right 1949–1950; (3) In decline 1951–1953. She rejected this idea because it was less suitable for her objectives in the speech.

A supreme merit of planning your speech in this way is that it forces this kind of discipline on you. It makes you reject unsuitable ideas. We shall see this again in the Middle section, but it is especially important to use the discipline now in choosing the main themes. They are the fundamental architecture of the speech, and if you get them wrong your speech will be badly built.

The Middle

The Middle section is of course the main body of the speech, adding the necessary detail to support and embellish its main themes. This is where you put most of the facts to inform, the arguments to persuade, the passages to make people laugh and cry.

Yet again it is an excellent idea to plan it by threes: three sub-themes for each main theme. What is a sub-theme? It depends on the primary purpose of your speech. It might be a group of facts, or a supporting argument, or an illustrative story, or something built on a visual aid, or even, in an entertaining speech, a single joke or one-liner.

The length of each sub-theme will obviously depend on the time you have available for the Middle.

We saw at the beginning of this chapter that in a 20-minute speech you have at most 15 minutes for the Middle. So if you have three times three sub-themes, making nine, each one has (on average) 15/9 minutes = 100 seconds.

A normal rate of speech is 150 words a minute, and you will frequently have to slow that down, for complex passages, for anything including numbers, for anything you really want people to remember. You might sometimes speak quicker than 150 words a minute, when telling a joke or developing a sweeping emotional passage – but then of course you will have to pause for laughter, applause or passionate cries of support from your audience. So it is right to think of 150 words a minute as a maximum. Therefore with 100 seconds per sub-theme, each has a maximum of 250 words. How much is 250 words? The following passage is.

"'The buck stops here.' You have probably heard that saying many times. It was first said by Harry Truman. It derives from poker (Harry Truman loved poker) and refers to the moment when each player has to make a decision which no one else can make.

Harry Truman loved making decisions. Sometimes he consulted other people, sometimes he took them alone, but he never asked anyone else to take responsibility or blamed anyone else for their consequences. In this sense he was always alone when he took his big decisions – dropping the atom bombs on Japan, pursuing civil rights at home, standing up to Stalin in Europe, fighting the Korean war, firing Douglas Macarthur – and he never lost a night's sleep.

Truman was also alone in a more practical sense. His personal staff in the White House never amounted to more than 13 people. No disrespect to our current President, who has over a thousand, but Harry Truman created the modern United States and the modern world with at most 13 people. And not one of them was an opinion pollster or a spin doctor. Truman never cared about opinion polls or media comment. He never had anyone to plant things in the media. He gave direct answers to questions and if you read a transcript of a Truman press conference you will always see him giving this kind of answer:

a big decision, a simple explanation followed by another characteris-
tic Truman expression 'And that's all there is to it.'**"**

That is exactly 250 words. In a 20-minute speech that should be your maximum length for a sub-theme. In a longer speech you will obviously have
more room for each sub-theme, and you can obviously create more room in
a shorter speech by cutting some sub-themes or dropping them altogether.
But in most cases 250 words will be quite enough for each sub-theme. The
passage above does not need anything more to convince an audience that
Truman was a decisive president. If the speaker added something else, however brilliant, the audience would start to get restive.

If you know or care anything about your subject, it is certain that you will
have too much material for the Middle of your speech. Here again the planning process and the rule of three will help you to select what is right for
you.

Begin by jotting down everything which might be a sub-theme to each main
theme. In the Truman speech it might look like this:

```
How Truman changed USA
● economy
● baby boom
● labour relations
● full employment
● civil rights/desegregation
● consumer boom (cars, TV, housing)
● farmers R? farm policy impact on town
● exports, dominance global economy
● 1948 election
● anti-Communism, McCarthy, security issues
● preserves presidency (Macarthur fired)
```

This list is clearly too long. It must come down to three and there are three
ways to do this. Collapse some candidates into each other; assign some candidates to another main theme; drop some candidates altogether.

'Baby boom' and 'consumer boom' can be collapsed into 'economy'. 'Full
employment' and 'labour relations' might go together, but that would give

'labour relations' only a share of the 250 words of a sub-theme. It is too complicated to fit into that space. A better plan is to put 'full employment' into the economy sub-theme and drop 'labour relations' altogether.

'Exports' could easily be reassigned to the second main theme of Truman changing the world. '1948 election' and 'preserves presidency' could go with the third main theme, the Truman model of leadership.

That leaves three candidates fighting for two places as sub-themes. 'Civil rights' is a must. 'Farmers' wins over 'anti-communism' because it was more relevant locally (and, as it happens, a more successful aspect of Truman's presidency).

The plan and the rule of three have forced the speaker to make decisions and leave things out. The discarded candidates should not disappear completely – they should go automatically on a list for topics to be prepared for Questions and Answers. The relevant part of the plan now looks like this:

```
1. How Truman changed USA
   (a) economy
       • growth
       • full employment
       • baby boom (Clinton, George W. Bush)
       • consumer (cars, TV, housing R? % US homes
         built in Truman years)
   (b) farmers R? impact on town
   (c) civil rights/desegregation

2. How Truman changed the world
   (a) exports, dominance global economy

3. The Truman model of leadership
   (a) 1948 election
   (b) preserves presidency (Macarthur fired)
```

Exactly the same process must now happen with the second and third main themes – collapsing sub-themes, reassigning or discarding. Obviously it gets more and more difficult to reassign, since themes 1 and 2 will run out of parking space. However, the planning process will still do its job of forcing you to choose the right material for your speech.

When the process is complete, the final plan for the Truman Middle section might look like this:

1. How Truman changed USA
   (a) economy
      - growth
      - full employment
      - baby boom (Clinton, George W. Bush)
      - consumer (cars, TV, housing <u>R? % US homes built in Truman years</u>)
   (b) farmers <u>R? impact on town</u>
   (c) civil rights/desegregation

2. How Truman changed world
   (a) containment of Communism (Marshall Plan, NATO, delayed victory 1989 fall of Berlin Wall)
   (b) economic superpower (incl Third World aid)
   (c) Israel

3. The Truman model of leadership
   (a) Buck stops here — decision-maker (A bombs, confront Stalin, civil rights, Korea, — 13 staff!)
   (b) plain speaking (1948 election, letter to music critic)
   (c) preserves powerful presidency (Congress, Cabinet, Macarthur)

Questions and Answers
- labour relations
- anti-Communism/security
- China
- origins Korean war
- what if Truman had lost 1948?

This plan will almost certainly produce a successful speech. It will need some flexibility (the economy will need to seize some space from farmers) but it will certainly keep the speaker focused on her main themes and prevent her wasting any time on irrelevancies. It will also make it much easier to write the Middle – the bulk of the speech.

I have made only glancing references so far to visual aids. We will be looking at them in a later chapter. At this point it is worth noting simply that if you intend to rely heavily on a visual aid or a sequence of them you need to incorporate them into your plan. Code them in a way that makes them unmistakeable and makes clear where they are going to be used. Here's an example in a plan for a speech on the early history of London's Metropolitan Police force.

> 1. Crime in London early C19th
>   - (a) high crime areas   V1 MAP LONDON 1825
>   - (b) social problems   V2 PRINT GIN DRINKER
>   - (c) organized crime   V3 PRINT BILL SYKES
>
> 2. Policing in London
>   - (a) private patrols
>   - (b) Peel in government   V4 CARTOON PEEL
>   - (c) Met Police founded 1829   V5 PRINT 'PEELER IN UNIFORM'

As we shall see in Chapter 13, this speaker is using too many visual aids, but at least he or she knows where to put them.

The End

The end of your speech is easy to plan but less easy to execute. Write the plan backwards, so that the first entry is:

Do your job

It is surprisingly easy to forget that speech may have a specific purpose. I have seen many speakers deliver a rousing finish, acknowledge the ecstatic audience and sit down, only to stand up again moments later, awkward and embarrassed, to propose the toast, move the vote, or nominate the nominee.

Even if your speech does not have a specific context like a dinner or a debate, it will always have some basic objective. Go back to the last chapter and look again at the aims of your speech and the desired outcome from your audience. The last words of your speech must achieve them. Doing your job might be helped by a visual aid – for example, to help the audience write down an address or a website. If so, make a note on the plan:

```
Do your job V7 SLIDE WITH ADDRESS
```

Now again working backwards write down:

```
Strong finish
Do your job
```

A great number of speeches peter out because the speaker has not thought about a strong finish. He or she suddenly becomes aware that time is up, or that the audience is restive, and bumbles some apologetic remark about taking up so much time or keeping them away from the bar. I have heard some speakers actually apologize for not thinking up an ending.

Some speeches do not peter out but simply drop dead.

The End is the last thing people will remember about you. Why let them remember that you are incompetent?

Some speeches do not peter out but simply drop dead. The speaker finishes a point and suddenly sits down. This invariably mystifies and annoys an audience and guarantees that the people who have not been listening will not remember anything at all.

So remind yourself to create a strong finish – something to wake up the sleepers, refocus the daydreamers and give everyone in the audience the memory and the mood you want them to take away. The strong finish is no place for a visual aid, which will simply compete with you. Now write down on the plan:

```
Recap
Strong finish
Do your job
```

The End should recapitulate your major themes, as snappily as possible. Finally write down on the plan:

```
Warning
Recap
Strong finish
Do your job
```

It is a very good idea to warn your audience that the End is Nigh. It will cheer them up and make them pay attention. The warning can be very brief. There is nothing wrong with the words 'In conclusion . . .'.

Here is a more detailed plan for the End of a debating speech against the euro:

```
Warning
Recap
    • euro threat to health, education, public services
    • euro threat to jobs
    • euro threat to democracy

Strong finish
    Opponents offer bromides, soft soap. Audience not
    fooled. Don't give up power. Reject euro

Do your job
    Vote against motion
```

It worked – the motion was lost.

When you have completed a detailed plan in this way, you will probably notice one other benefit. The plan should do nicely as your speaking notes. We will come later to whether you should speak from a full text or from notes. The broad answer is that you speak from the full text if it is vital that you put it on the record word for word, without deviation. Otherwise you will get more atmosphere and more contact with the audience by using a route map of your speech, with the key arguments and facts. Your plan will do that for you.

SUMMARY

- Your speech needs a plan. The more you plan the better it will be, and the easier it will be to write it.
- Your plan needs an Introduction, a Beginning, a Middle and an End.

- In the Introduction, plan to thank everyone you need to and to con-nect with your audience.

- A safe and effective way to connect with any audience is to praise the host organization, the setting and, if appropriate, the locality. You may be able to do this and simultaneously deliver a key mes-sage.

- While making your plan, flag up points you need to research.

- Your Beginning needs a 'grabber' – something which makes your audience pay attention.

- In a debate, your Beginning should deal first with any previous opposing speakers.

- After the grabber, the Beginning should state your main themes – a maximum of three.

- The Middle – the bulk of your speech – is built around your three main themes. Plan sub-themes for each main theme – a maxi-mum of three each.

- A sub-theme means any organized material which supports a main theme. It can be as short as a single joke or one-liner. Work out the time and length you can afford to give each sub-theme.

- Use your plan to choose the most relevant sub-themes and organize them in the most effective way.

- Use discarded sub-themes to suggest answers to prepare for questions.

- In the End, plan to warn people that it is nigh, repeat your main themes, create a strong finish and do the specific job of your speech.

- Make precise entries in the plan for any visual aids.

- The completed plan should do admirably as speaking notes.

5

Writing it down: talking it out

Preparing a full text

Having prepared an admirable plan, it is very tempting not to write out your speech. You will now know what you want to say and you may well feel confident that you can speak to the plan.

Resist the temptation. You must write your speech in full. Apart from any other reason, you may want to publish it or at least give a written copy to your host organization. A High Impact Speech must be composed, every word from 'Thank you' to 'Vote for Me', even if you intend to deliver it from notes.

You must write your speech in full.

Writing out a full text is the only way you will be able to time yourself properly, both the whole speech and individual segments. Without writing out your speech it is all too easy to get excited by your first point, speak on it at length, and discover that you have only two minutes left for everything else. Writing your speech in full will help you cut out ers and ums and infuriating empty expressions like . . . like . . . you know . . .

Writing your speech in full will stop you losing your way in a sentence, it's when you start with one thing and suddenly think of another, there are speakers like this, it's absolutely infuriating to audiences – like being driven by someone who's lost – I can't remember but it was some politician maybe American that said 'I can go fifteen minutes without a verb' which is the problem to be faced.

Writing a full text will give you discipline, forcing you constantly to make your points in the most effective way. It will give you automatic feedback: if you speak your words as you write them you will pick up basic errors, like poor grammar or gobbledygook or accidental laughs. ('The Queen greeted Tony Blair wearing a long blue dress and a tiara.')

If you need a famous example, think of Winston Churchill. He spent six to eight hours on each of his wartime speeches, composing them word for word, checking and revising them two or three times, and finally having them written out as he meant to say them, in a special format modelled on the Psalms of the Bible. Churchill did all this in the midst of running a nation at war. The result of this effort is history.

Churchill did have one great advantage: he dictated his speeches. He wrote and talked at the same time. This is an invaluable technique. *Writing and talking your speech simultaneously* will tell you whether your words are fitting together well, and when they are it will give you fluency, momentum and excitement.

One American president was allegedly unable to walk and chew gum at the same time. Some people cannot seem to write and talk at the same time and that explains 95.7 per cent of all the speeches that go wrong. (How do I know it is 95.7 per cent? I don't. It is a very old trick to use a very precise number to make people stop and think – see the section in Chapter 8, 'Numbers are metaphors'.)

It is helpful to think of a speech as a conversation. I remember hearing Mrs Barbara Bush, the popular First Lady, address the Republican Convention of 1992. She told the massed ranks of delegates, and **Some people cannot** the vast television audience: 'I'm not going to give you **seem to write and** a speech today. I'm going to have a conversation with **talk at the same time.** you.' (She then of course delivered a short, brilliantly crafted *speech* which brought home her down-to-earth personality.) Mrs Bush was right. The great majority of speeches are con-versation with the audience, for all that one party is doing the talking. A speech is a very concentrated form of conversation, in that writing and rehearsal have wiped out unnecessary words and deviations, but it uses no techniques which people do not use in ordinary conversation. A speech argues, informs, rouses emotion in just the same ways that people do in conversation. Later on, when we look at 'figures of speech' and other tech-nical concepts you will find that you have been using all of them all of your life.

A few speeches, by the truly great, do break the bound-aries of conversation. Their words develop a surge of rhythm and music and emotion which is akin to poetry. Martin Luther King's 'I Have a Dream' speech is a famous example, with its Biblical cadences, flowing sentences and deliberate repetitions. Yet when it was delivered, King drew his biggest response from everyday conversational images (travelling on a bus, drinking a cup of coffee in a restaurant), rather than his more elevated, abstract passages.

A speech is a very concentrated form of conversation.

In writing-and-talking you can therefore apply two simple tests for any pas-sage, any word. Would I use this in a conversation? Could I put this into a poem? Now apply this test to a recent speech by a British government min-ister:

"Democratically-elected councils should be part of the fabric of our communities. The services they provide have a vital part to play in sustaining and enhancing the social and economic prospects and environmental quality of our towns, cities and countryside.

They can have a profound effect on the opportunities and quality of life of the people who live and work there: educating children, pro-viding care for the vulnerable, making places safer and cleaner to live in, and providing reliable local transport.

People therefore expect a great deal from their council. And those expectations are rising. To meet them, councils have constantly to seek new and more effective ways to deliver customer-focused serv-ices and lead their communities."

(Rt Hon Stephen Byers MP, then Secretary of State for Transport, Local Government and the Regions, 11 December 2001)

There is nothing wrong with this in content or clarity. But strike out any-thing you would not use in a normal conversation. Strike out anything you would not try to fit into a poem. Not much of it survives, although you may have discovered that 'customer-focused services' can be chanted to the same rhythm as 'Here we go gathering nuts in May'. These struck-out pas-sages are what make the speech a failure. They put the speaker in another world from his audience.

(I have to admit that this test is not as clear-cut as it used to be. There are a growing number of people who actually use phrases like 'deliver customer-focused services' in everyday conversation. But they are still exceptional. If you want a speech to reach 'normal' people you listen as you write and imagine yourself talking to them in a 'normal' setting. This will ensure that you deliver customer-focused phrases.)

After a while, you should not need to test your writing so formally. Writing-and-talking will warn you automatically when something is wrong. Writing-and-talking is so easy you can do it without writing. Any time you like you can compose passages and talk them through to yourself.

When you see people in public transport with a strange, spaced-out expression and their lips moving, do not be alarmed. They are probably speech-writers.

Writing-and-talking will warn you automatically when something is wrong.

The technique of writing-and-talking is even more vital if you are writing for someone else. You must talk through every passage in his or her voice. This is terribly hard, but it is your duty. Passages which may seem normal and conversational, or brilliant and poetic to you, could be stilted or mangled in another person's voice. You must keep alert for individual mannerisms and you must consider constantly whether any material fits your speaker's general style and character.

Edward Heath, who was Britain's Prime Minister in the early 1970s, had notorious difficulty with the sound 'ow'. He tended to turn it into a dipthong 'ee-yow'. He was given a draft of a speech in which he was predicting success in a political contest. It ended 'I have no dee-yowt ab-ee-yowt the ee-owtcome.' That speech-writer did not last very long.

If you are writing for another, it is always fatal to force him or her to adopt a different personality as a speaker. I remember the efforts speech-writers made to make former Vice-President Dan Quayle sound like an intellectual heavyweight. They backfired and redoubled the mockery which was being thrown at the Vice-President. In British politics, the same error was made when people tried to make former Labour leader Michael Foot sound like a master of economics, and when they try to make the present Deputy Prime Minister, John Prescott, sound like a managerial technocrat.

And I weep for all the speech-writers who tried to make Margaret Thatcher tell a joke.

Blocked?

One of the hidden advantages of writing-and-talking is that it helps to overcome writer's block. Most people talk faster and more fluently than they write and they can usually hear themselves a few sentences ahead of the writing on the page. This drives forward the writing process and whole pages fill up delightfully quickly.

However, people do sometimes run out of conversation, even when they are talking to themselves. They hear nothing, the written page catches up with their last sentence and then dries up altogether.

There are several ways to deal with writer's block. First, remember that it is quite temporary. Inspiration will come back, you will soon be writing-and-talking to yourself again. Drop the speech. Do something physical. If you are at home, do some housework or gardening (if you write at home, there will always be neglected jobs at home or in the garden). If you are stir-crazy, walk, run or take a bike ride or a swim: take a child with you, if available. At least do the shopping. If you are blocked in the office, leave it for as long as you can, and do something active. At all costs do not think about the

Drop the speech. Do something physical.

speech. If you concentrate on the activity, the words will come back to your head and you will notice yourself talking to yourself again. Do not rush back to the speech but continue the activity to get full value from the stimulus.

A burst of activity removes most blockages but if it fails, do not go back to the speech. Instead do the most boring task in your in-tray. Do your income tax, or reply to the stupid memo from higher management. Again, you should find yourself talking your speech and again, do not rush back to it, but finish the boring task.

You may be up against a very tight deadline and cannot afford the time for activity or boredom therapy. You still have time for a micro-nap, or shutting your eyes and visiting your favourite place. If that does not release you, try the method of the American novelist, Edna Ferber. Start a new page, type your address and then the words 'Dear Mom . . .'

Alcohol, caffeine, nicotine and other chemicals are not cures to writer's block.

If you cannot think of anything to put in a letter to your mother, you are in trouble. You will have to go back to your speech and be a brave little soldier. Force yourself to write something. Don't be too self-critical. It may not be up to the standard you want but it is filling the page and helping you meet the deadline. Remember when you took exams. Writing something gives you some chance of a pass, writing nothing is an automatic fail.

Alcohol, caffeine, nicotine and other chemicals are not cures to writer's block.

SUMMARY

- You must write out every speech in full, even if you intend to deliver it from notes.

- Develop the technique of writing-and-talking simultaneously.

- Imagine words and passages as part of a normal conversation, or as part of a poem.

- If you are writing for another, talk every word through in his or her voice.

- If you get writer's block, leave the speech and do something active or boring. At least escape for a few moments. In desperation, force yourself to write something, even if you think it is poor.

Tricks and techniques: simple speech and weird words

Create effects by changing styles of language

In the last chapter we talked about the art of listening to yourself as you write your speech. In the next few chapters we are going to examine some familiar techniques and tricks. The next three chapters are relevant for all speeches; the one after (Chapter 9) is especially relevant to arguing and persuading.

Many of these techniques have technical names, particularly those which are formally classed as 'figures of speech'. However, there is nothing out-landish about any of them. I am certain that you will find that you have used all of them in ordinary conversation and ordinary argument – or heard them used by someone else to work on you.

As we run through each example, talk it through to yourself. Think of a time when you spoke like that yourself. Think of a time when you heard someone else speak like that. Did it work *for* you? Did it work *against* you? You will then be able to concentrate more in your writing on the tricks and techniques which work and avoid the ones which fail.

Of course if you are writing for someone else, you will apply the first test in a different way if you know your intending speaker at all. You will men-tally replay your speaker in ordinary conversation and you will remember perhaps that he or she is brilliant at delivering the 'killer fact' but makes a dog's dinner of metaphors. If you like your job, you will then write speeches with plenty of killer facts and no metaphors.

All of these tricks and techniques are designed to make you more like the person you are. (Or to make your speaker more like himself or herself.)

That is what you can learn from the failures. When you talk through the ones that failed to work *for* you (your chosen speaker), you will almost certainly find that they did not fit well with your (his, her) core personality.

You may learn something even more interesting when you talk through the tricks and techniques which failed when someone else tried to use them *against* you. Very often, that will have happened **Why imitate people** because you associate this trick or technique with **you dislike?** someone you dislike, or a class of person you dislike or distrust. It will then be a good idea to cut this trick or technique from your speaking repertoire. Why imitate people you dislike? If you dislike them, your audience will probably dislike them too.

Avoid bad associations

In particular there are some familiar rhetorical devices which have become devalued through association with unpopular groups of people – especially 'slick' politicians or salespeople.

One is called '*defining the background*'. This used to be a very effective way of dealing with an awkward fact or argument. Before analyzing or even presenting that fact or argument, the speaker would give the audience a background of different facts which made them see the awkward fact in a different light. Unfortunately, this ancient technique has become a politician's trick which conveys an impression of insincerity or even outright dishonesty. For example, British politicians are frequently challenged to respond to individual disasters in the National Health Service. All too frequently they reply with something like this: 'This is a tragic case, but before we discuss it in detail I think it is important that I set out the background to the government's health policy. We are spending . . . per cent more in real terms on the National Health Service than the last government, there are . . . more doctors, . . . more nurses, and hospital waiting lists are down by . . . since we took office. Next year we shall be spending . . .'

People have heard this kind of argument so often from politicians that it rarely works. They no longer accept a background defined by politicians: they probably will not accept it from you.

Another devalued technique is that of *'answering the opposite question'*. Again it used to work well. When a speaker had an awkward question to answer he would ask the exactly opposite question and show that it had an even more awkward answer. Unfortunately this technique has become associated with high-pressure salespeople. The former Labour leader Neil Kinnock was one of the last great orators in British politics. But I once heard him wreck a major economic broadcast with a misplaced use of this technique. Discussing a rather expensive economic plan by his party, Mr Kinnock spelt out its benefits and then said, 'I am sometimes asked: can we afford to do it? My question is: can we afford *not* to do it?' Millions of people in his audience would have remembered that argument from a salesperson – and remembered buying something bad and expensive as a result.

Constantly think: where have I heard that before?

So if you want to avoid sounding like a high-pressure salesperson, you should think carefully before you use this technique.

In the coming chapters I will try to give some health warnings on tricks and techniques which may have acquired harmful associations. But your own experience will do that job much better. Constantly think: where have I heard that before? If it is an unpleasant memory do not do it again.

Don't give yourself airs

Asking that question will also stop you falling into the opposite peril – evoking associations which are, frankly, too good for you. Some tricks and techniques are associated with truly great orators and it is presumptious and annoying to an audience to put yourself in their place. For example, deliberate repetition can be very effective – beginning a series of sentences with exactly the same phrase. But if it makes you (or your speaker) sound like Martin Luther King, forget it. The device will make an audience concentrate on the *difference* between you (or your speaker) and Martin Luther King, not the similarity.

Winston Churchill is another dangerous example. Like Martin Luther King he was fond of deliberate repetition, but he had other personal tricks (like the use of double adjectives) which gave his speeches a special rhythm and richness. Test these tricks by all means, but if they turn you (or your speaker) into a parody Churchill, leave them behind on the cutting room floor.

Keeping in mind all those necessary warnings, you are now ready to test-drive some of the motors of good writing and speaking.

When to keep it simple

Almost every manual of good writing and good speaking will tell you to use everyday language. They will suggest that you use the simplest and commonest words which convey your meaning. They advise you to prefer short words to long ones, to prefer Saxon words to Latin, to **Don't get weird.** prefer modern expressions to old-fashioned ones. They will warn you against straining for effect. They will tell you to avoid technical language, jargon and gobbledygook. You could summarize all this advice in three words: don't get weird.

This is extremely good advice. It is right far more often than it is wrong. Simple, everyday language conveys your meaning more effectively than pompous circumlocutions and connects you instantly to your audience. It may also save you from making a fool of yourself. Some years ago, the then American ambassador to London, Walter Annenberg, was voted Britain's most popular television comedian, after his appearance in a TV documentary about the Queen. She asked him if he had moved into his residence. Perhaps flustered in the presence of majesty, Mr Annenburg replied: 'In present circumstances, ma'am, we are suffering from elements of discomfiture associated with factors of refurbishing about the residency.' He meant 'We've got the builders in.'

Mr Annenburg was an amateur. Since his time we have seen the rise of professional obscurantists, people who deliberately say nothing at all in a great number of complex words. Many are government bureaucrats, others are professionals who use jargon as a claim to expertise. Lawyers, priests, soldiers, alchemists, astrologers are ancient professions which quickly invented their own special language, but their efforts have been overtaken by the twentieth century's priesthood: economists, psychologists, social scientists and management consultants. I do not want to seem prejudiced (some of my best friends are management consultants) but some members of their profession are jargonaholics.

In England, managerial English brought a new eponym into the language – Birtspeak – named after its inventor, Sir John Birt. Ironically, he was Director-General of the BBC – one of the world's great communicators of English. Here is a prime sample: 'We need to establish a less prescriptive corporate framework which offers business units greater flexibility within the parameters of common core corporate guidelines.'[1]

We have seen the rise of professional obscurantists.

People sometimes use long words in speeches because they think that they sound better, and may give their speech some grandeur and poetry. In fact it is non-complex discourse which has the operational capability for optimal euphony, that is to say, simple language sounds better and it is easier to create special effects with it. Because simple words are easy to say you can use them to build pace and rhythm in a speech and to change the pace and rhythm deliberately when you want to. Here is a famous example:

> **"We shall not flag or fail. We shall go on to the end, we shall fight in France, we shall fight on the seas and oceans, we shall fight with growing confidence and growing strength in the air, we shall defend our island, whatever the cost may be, we shall fight on the beaches, we shall fight on the landing grounds, we shall fight in the fields and in the streets, we shall fight in the hills; we shall never surrender."**

Winston Churchill used nothing but everyday words in that passage but they produce an electrifying effect. The words gather pace but they slow down when Churchill wants them to (for example, when he wants listeners to think a little longer about the fight in the air). They change their rhythm and create a near-rhyme to deliver the key message: 'We shall defend our island, whatever the cost may be.'

If Birtspeak had been around in 1940, Churchill's speech might have expressed as: 'There is no template of diminution or dysfunction. We shall

---

[1] Quoted in C. Horrie and S. Clarke, *Fuzzy Monsters* (London, 1994).

continue in our strategic policy framework until we have delivered all of our objectives going forward in all of our chosen operational theatres, in both overseas and domestic locations, we shall achieve our mission and reject any sub-optimal outcome.' And Hitler might have won the war.

When to be weird

Although it is nearly always right to use simple, everyday language, some famous speakers have used deliberately used exotic, unusual language.

Lincoln's Gettysburg address appears in virtually everyone's list of the best speeches in history. It is often held out as a model of simplicity. Yet it begins with unusual language, which would have sounded archaic even in 1863. 'Four score and seven years ago . . .' Lincoln might have said, in everyday terms, 'Eighty-seven years ago'. He chose to say 'Four score and seven'. The words do sound more solemn and stately, and Lincoln was speaking at a memorial ceremony for those killed in war. But there was a deeper reason for his choice. 'Four score and seven' is the language of the Bible, the best-known book in the United States. By evoking the Bible, Lincoln made a claim on its authority and, even more important, connected instantly with his audience.

Sometimes you may not want to make your audience comfortable but to shock them.

By all means, follow Lincoln's example. If a complex, ornate, unusual, expression does a better job *for your audience* than an everyday one, by all means use it. For example, if you were speaking to an audience of chemists they will probably respond better to scientific terms rather than everyday ones. They will actually prefer 'sodium chloride' to 'common salt'.

An audience of management gurus will be perfectly comfortable with management words. Read at the end of this book the excerpt from the speech by Jon Moynihan, the Chairman of PA Consulting Group. It was a motivational speech of welcome for new recruits to this leading consultancy. It uses several jargon phrases which you will be advised to cut in Chapter 10. Why did Mr Moynihan get away with it? Because of his audience – a group perfectly at ease with 'client-focused'. His speech met the basic test – it was, in its context, a conversation.

Sometimes you may not want to make your audience comfortable but to shock them, or at least to manipulate them into a particular response. Sometimes you may simply want them to stop and think. An unusual word might do these jobs for you better than an everyday one.

Later in Churchill's famous speech in 1940 he suddenly uses an exotic word after a long passage of simple ones: 'and even if, which I do not for a moment believe, this island or a large part of it, were **subjugated** and starving . . .' There were plenty of everyday words available in place of 'subjugated'. Churchill might have used 'beaten' or 'defeated' or 'conquered', or if he was determined to have an alliteration with 'starving' he might have used 'suppressed'. But none of these would have stopped his listeners as effectively as the four syllables of 'subjugated'. With the unusual word, Churchill made people think a little longer about what it might mean to be conquered by the Nazis: 'subjugated' has overtones of abasement and enslavement and Churchill wanted his listeners to hear them.

So when is it right to be weird? When you have a weird audience, or when weird language lets you claim a special connection with your audience, or when you want your audience to think or act in a weird way.

Loaded language

There is one special category of weirdness in speech-making – when you deliberately use loaded language. Simple, everyday words rarely carry emotional baggage. They are the couriers of the English language: they get to their destination as fast as possible, deliver the message and hurry away to their next assignment. But if you want your messenger to deliver flowers as well, and wait for the right reply, you need a specialized message service.

Loaded language uses slightly special words, which say 'Hooray!' or 'Boo!' as soon as they are uttered. We had an example in the Introduction, in the speech by Huxley against Bishop 'Soapy' Sam Wilberforce: 'rhetoric' was a Boo! word (so, of course, are the words 'Soapy Sam').

Not surprisingly, politicians are especially adept at using Hooray! and Boo! words. Many receive elaborate coaching on words to avoid, words to use and words to pin on their opponents. For example, few politicians in the English-speaking world will talk about 'public spending'. At best that is a neutral expression, and 'spending' has some negative connotations. The Hooray! expression is 'investment in public services'.

In politics, words often travel in pairs, in a Boo! version and a Hooray! version. Examples are 'elitist' (Boo!) and 'expert' (Hooray!), or 'bureaucrat' (Boo!) and 'public servant' (Hooray!), 'repressive' (Boo!) and 'tough' (Hooray!). If you like another country's rulers they are its 'government', if you are uncertain about them they are its 'administration', and if you cannot stand them they are its 'regime'.

Perhaps under the influence of politics, the same kind of pairing is increasingly frequent in ordinary speech. Think of 'simple' (generally a Hooray!) and 'simplistic' (Boo!), 'easy' (neutral or Hooray!) and 'facile' (Boo!) or 'flexible' (Hooray!) and 'pliable' (Boo!): politicians who are fond of the buzzword 'flexible labour markets' might try the effect of substituting 'pliable labour markets'.

You can get more of a Boo! or Hooray! effect with a strange word rather than a commonplace one.

Quite often you can get more of a Boo! or Hooray! effect with a strange word rather than a commonplace one. Calling someone 'oily' is pretty insulting, but call him 'oleaginous' to express real contempt. 'Woolly thinking' is bad enough but 'flocculent thinking' (with its echo of 'flatulence') is far more pejorative. Another strange word with a useful echo is 'inspissated' (it means thickened or condensed, as in Campbell's Inspissated Soup) and it works well in conjunction with words like 'gloom' or 'tedium' or 'obscurity'.

Sometimes a foreign word carries more Boo! or Hooray! than an English one. 'Bureaucrat' is quite a wounding expression but 'apparatchik' is positively venomous. When I toiled in British politics as a dingy researcher I often borrowed a title from French politics as a more glamorous job description: 'chef de cabinet'. If you are ever stuck for a colourful expression I recommend the Yiddish language. Why call someone a 'mediocrity' when you can call him a 'nebbish', a 'schlemiel' or a 'nudnik'?

When no current word, English or foreign, is sufficiently loaded it can be very effective to make one up. An easy way to make up words is to tack on certain prefixes and suffixes. Common word-creating prefixes are Euro-, crypto- or mega- and mini-, and (pretentiously) uber-. Possible suffixes include -onomics, -ology, -otomy, -ocrat, -phile, -erast, -phobe, speak, -oholic, -naut, -ism, -ics, -ite and -ize. After Watergate, anything can be made into a scandal by adding -gate to it. Many of these work especially well when tacked on to a proper name. Yiddish offers the useful suffix -nik, usually pejorative (real estatenik, no-good-nik), occasionally complimentary (refusenik).

> **An easy way to make up words is to tack on certain prefixes and suffixes.**

However, as a result of newspapers this form of word creation is becoming dangerously close to cliché, especially the use of -gate. You might instead prefer to make a slight switch on a familiar expression. My old boss Denis Healey did this to brilliant effect 20 years ago in British politics when he called Mrs Thatcher's economic policy 'sado-monetarism'. The term was so successful that it passed into international use, to describe the deflationary policies of other right-wing leaders. More recently I enjoyed the term 'apathexy', to describe voters who are not only indifferent to the political process but positively repelled by it.

A few months ago the British Home Secretary, David Blunkett, found a new word as a blanket insult to all the critics of his anti-terrorist laws. Rather than use the now cliché term 'kneejerk liberals' he branded them the 'Liberati' conveying the same message with (for him) the useful added suggestion that they were foreign. (He might have made it still more insulting by calling them the Gliberati.)

New and strange words work as loaded language only if they have associations *for your audience*. When you try them out, be your audience listening to you. Are they intrigued or excited – or irritated by your affectations? If in doubt, cut them out (see Chapter 10, 'All your little darlings must be killed').

To sum up, loaded language is a context in which you *may* succeed with a weird expression (even one you have invented). A weird expression can work not only because of its novelty, but because it will almost certainly change the pace of your speech. You will slow down when you say it, either for relish or simply to be sure of saying it properly, which means that your audience will have to slow down with you and (you hope) concentrate a little harder on your meaning.

SUMMARY

- Speech-makers and speech-writers use many special tricks and techniques – but they are all used regularly in ordinary conversation.

- When you try out any trick or technique, talk it through and try to remember when you used it or heard it in ordinary life. If you are writing for someone else, imagine him or her using that trick or technique in conversation.

- Be careful before you use tricks or techniques which have bad associations – and good associations.

- Plain, simple, everyday, jargon-free language is nearly always right, and can easily take off into poetry.

- But you may use 'weird' language to reach a 'weird' audience or make an ordinary audience respond in a special way.

- Unusual, foreign and invented words can sometimes carry an especially loaded message.

Tricks and techniques: getting familiar with your audience

How to make things clear

One of the commonest tasks in any speech is to make something obscure sound familiar to the audience.

Something can be obscure to an audience for two reasons. First, they may not know much about it at all (Tibetan Buddhism, the sex life of the sea urchin, the long-range business cycle). Second, although they may know quite a lot about it (marriage, children, crime) they may not know what you think about it.

> **One of the commonest tasks in any speech is to make something obscure sound familiar to the audience.**

You may simply want them to understand the obscure thing, or you may also want them to respond to it intellectually or emotionally.

You achieve this by building a logical relationship between the obscure thing and something familiar to your audience.

This can be very easy to do – so long as you remember. For example, if you are dealing with history, particularly remote history, you will do well to find a valid contemporary comparison. I once heard a lecturer make a vivid comparison between Alfred the Great (reigned 871–899) and Tony Blair (reigned 1997–). If you are quoting the price of something in history (or someone's earnings) you should translate it into today's money. In this context, history means five years old or more.

If you have to mention a very big number, you should find some way of dividing it to make it familiar to your audience. A six-figure number (i.e. hundreds of thousands) is the largest that most people will deal with in their ordinary lives – when they buy or sell their house. If you have a bigger number in your speech which represents so much per year, you could divide it by 52 or 365 to get it down to so much per week or per day. (A week will often work better than a day as a comparator, because many people still budget by the week.) You might also try dividing your big number by 60 million (in the UK) or 280 million (in the USA) and expressing it as so much 'for every man, woman and child in the country'.

If for some reason you cannot divide the big number you may have to compare it to something familiar to your audience. Think about whether you want your audience to be impressed with the bigness of the number or its smallness. In the first case you might try 'double the annual cost of the National Health Service'. In the second case, you might say 'half of what our nation spends on dog food each year'. (We shall be looking at this point again in the section Chapter 8, 'Numbers are metaphors'). If you have to convey the size of something by a number compare it to something familiar (three football pitches, or better still four times taller than this hall).

I always feel sorry for astronomers who have to deal with colossal numbers. They often make desperate efforts to scale down their numbers to familiar dimensions ('imagine the sun is this blown-up beachball, and earth is a Brussels sprout ten feet away with this dried pea revolving round it, and Jupiter is this apricot . . .'). If your numbers are so unreal, do not try to explain them – leave them as they are and hope that your audience will be suitably awed.

In many branches of science it is often possible to explain a principle by giving a vivid everyday example of it in action. A chemist might explain the principle of oxidation by showing how things rust. An economist might explain the economics of scarcity with the example of black market tickets for major sports games and rock concerts.

In the speech in the Appendix to this book 'Cheaper by the Gallon', the Chairman of Texaco, Alfred C. Decrane, Jr, had to explain to his audience some complex advances in oil extraction technology. He made it much easier for them by referring constantly to aspects which were familiar and to related technologies which they were more likely to know. To give one example:

> **"Borrowing three-dimensional visualization software from the movie industry, we are now able to follow on a computer screen the flow of water, steam, carbon dioxide or chemicals that we inject into reservoirs to loosen the hydrocarbons and push them out."**

Few people in his audience would be familiar with computer imaging in oil extraction, but almost all of them would have seen it in the movies.

The art of analogy

History, numbers, science usually offer an easy way of turning the obscure into the familiar. More often, your task will be harder. You will have to think first of a good analogy. An analogy is a more complex form of comparison. In a simple comparison, you look at two or more things from the same category. (In my history example above, Alfred the Great and Tony Blair are far removed in time but they are in the same category – political leaders). In analogy, you look at two or more things which belong to different categories and see how one imitates the other.

An analogy is a more complex form of comparison

If you want to explain something obscure by analogy you therefore ask yourself: what is it in the everyday world which forms an accurate model or representation of the obscure thing?

It is surprising how many speakers perpetrate appalling analogies, using images of things which are nothing like the thing they want their audience to understand. I once heard a clergyman at a wedding service make an elaborate comparison of marriage to a cricket match. He was trying to please a congregation full of cricketers, but succeeded only in irritating them. The more he worked up the comparisons (sticking to the rules . . . accepting the umpire's decision . . .) the more obvious it became that cricket is nothing like marriage.

If your analogy is going to work for an audience, it must work not just on a verbal level (at best that will give you some weak jokes) but at a conceptual level. Although they come from different categories, the things compared should have the same logic and the same resonance.

If you have found a suitable analogy you must then find a good way to deliver it.

The simplest and quickest way is a vivid *simile* or *metaphor*. These are both figures of speech which compare unlike things with another. A simile connects them with words such as 'like' or 'as if': for example, 'his smile gleamed like the silver fittings on a coffin'. A metaphor dispenses with any connecting words – it melts unlike things into each other: 'he was my sun and moon, my east and west'.

We are going to look at similes and metaphors in a little more detail in Chapter 8 in the section on 'Fingers of speech'. At this point, I want to emphasize that they work best when they make a good analogy, by linking things which are conceptually the same.

George Orwell put a particularly brilliant metaphor and simile into his essay 'Politics and the English Language': 'an accumulation of stale phrases chokes him like tea leaves blocking a sink'. It takes his readers from something obscure, in the literary–political world (politically inspired clichés) to something familiar in the everyday world, and in a legitimate way – the clichés genuinely have the effect of something choking and blocking.

A longer method of delivering the comparison is by a joke or an anecdote. Essentially these are extended similes or metaphors. In both cases you are comparing something obscure with something familiar. With a simile or a metaphor, the familiar thing is a snapshot image, with a joke or an anecdote it is a movie. The same rule applies: the joke or anecdote works only if it delivers a fair comparison of one thing to another. If it does not, you will irritate your audience and you take the additional risk that your joke or anecdote takes longer to tell (see in Chapter 8 the section on 'Stop me if you have heard this before').

SUMMARY

- Things may be obscure to your audience because they do not know about them or because they do not know what you think of them. In either case, you must make them familiar.

- You can often make history familiar with the right contemporary comparison.

- Make numbers familiar by making them small or comparing them to something your audience understands.

- In science, you can often give an everyday example of a complicated idea or relate an unusual science to a more familiar one.

- You can use analogy to good effect – comparing something in an obscure category to something in a familiar category – but only if the analogy makes sense.

- A metaphor or simile is the quickest way to deliver a vivid, logical analogy. A joke or a story takes more time.

Tricks and techniques: variety and vitality

How to add colour, rhythm, pace and emotion

Earlier in this book, I advised you to be true to yourself. Speak in your natural style. I will now go back on this advice. If your natural style is monotonous, you really should try to find another one. (If you are writing for someone else who is monotonous, find something new for him or her.)

Anyone's speech will benefit from colour, rhythm, pace, emotion and, above all, variety. An audience cannot abide the same voice for too long. You can achieve all of these things, without being artificial and untrue to yourself. Here are some tricks and techniques which can help. As before, when you try them out you will probably find that you have used them or heard them frequently in ordinary life.

An audience cannot abide the same voice for too long.

As before, you should test them by ear – talk them through and hear yourself saying them (or hear the person you are writing for). But you can also test them usefully by eye. Look at your speech as it appears on the page. Can you see sentences and paragraphs of different lengths? If so, it is a healthy sign. A mix of long and short sentences and long and short paragraphs is a sign that your speech will have variety: in fact, it will virtually force you to give vocal interest to your speech and change the pitch and pace of your delivery.

I got rhythm

Every great speech contains rhythm, and more than one rhythm. As in music rhythm acts very strongly on the subconscious of listeners; it can make them excited or reflective, happy or angry, playful or serious and, above all, a strong rhythm keeps them in step with you.

Although there are particular devices which help to generate rhythm (notably repetition and using words in pairs) most speeches develop their rhythm by using simple words and using them *logically*. That means grouping words tightly, so that each group represents one complete thought. To illustrate this I took extra care over the last paragraph. If I break it down into its separate clauses and phrases, you should see that each one finishes off a particular thought and allows the next one to express another thought: *every great speech contains rhythm* and more than one rhythm. *As in music* rhythm acts very strongly on the subconscious of listeners; *it can make them excited or reflective,* happy or angry, *playful or serious* and, above all [not a thought but a warning to pay attention], *a strong rhythm keeps them in step with you.* It is not poetry, but that paragraph is easy to speak aloud.

Every great speech contains rhythm, and more than one rhythm.

I could have written that first paragraph differently as:

❝The presence of rhythm, and indeed of more than one rhythm, is a mark of every great speech. Rhythm, in terms of creating moods of excitement or reflection, happiness or anger, playfulness or seriousness, as in music, acts strongly on the subconscious of listeners. A strong rhythm, it should be emphasized, is instrumental in creating a strong linkage between listeners and yourself.❞

Try speaking that aloud. I have broken the link between ideas and groups of words, and forced you to reach the end of a meandering sentence before you know what you have said, and I have probably left you gasping for breath.

If you look again at my bad paragraph, you will notice that I severed the subject from the main verb. This is sheer cruelty: subjects and main verbs love being together and if you keep them together you will go a long way to creating happy, rhythmic sentences.

Other groups of words also like to be kept together, although not as passionately as subject and verb. If you have a group of words in a sentence which modifies its subject or its verb or its object it will probably read best if it stays close to the thing it modifies, and if it stays close to other groups of words doing the same job. Try out this sentence: 'Felix the Cat delighted American movie audiences, who recognized, in his endless ingenuity and unquenchable optimism, a kindred spirit and a symbol of the age.' I hope you find it jerky and unhappy. Try it again as: 'Endlessly ingenious and unquenchably optimistic, Felix the Cat delighted American movie audiences who recognized him as a kindred spirit and a symbol of the age.' I hope you find it flows better when the words modifying Felix are moved alongside him.

Subjects and main verbs love being together .

If any sentence does not seem to have the right rhythm, or any at all, try first cutting out the dead wood (see Chapter 10). If that has not cured the problem, try rearranging the word order until it does. It will probably make more sense as well.

Now read the passage by John Donne in the Appendix. Read it aloud. Donne was a great poet who also became a legendary preacher; the passage is part of a sermon to a packed congregation at old St Paul's. Notice the intense rhythms as you speak it, notice too how they are built on simple language. Notice in particular that Donne achieves his most dramatic change of rhythm by the five simplest words in the passage: 'now God comes to thee'. Notice finally that each cluster of words represents one thought, and that although many of the sentences are long the subjects are always close to their main verbs.

If you organize simple words logically, and listen to yourself as you do so, you should find yourself creating effective, rhythmic passages to speak. However if you are particularly interested in rhythm, you may find it worthwhile to do two special exercises.

The first is to mark the places in a passage of writing where you would expect you (or your speaker) to draw breath. They should fall at the end of a phrase or complete sentence, and, in a rhythmic passage, they should fall at regular intervals. A change in these intervals should mean a deliberate change of rhythm, but if the breathing intervals are all over the place then the speech has probably lost its rhythm.

The second is to write out the passage as lines of poetry. Go further and mark in the long and short syllables and where the main stresses fall. In a rhythmic passage you should see lines of a similar length, and some sort of pattern in the syllables and stresses.

Change of pace

Not surprisingly, most of the points we have just established about rhythm apply equally to pace. By using simple language logically you can achieve effective and essential changes of pace in your speech. However, there is one key difference. With rhythm you are working primarily with sound. But with pace you are also working with sense. Indeed, the whole point of changing the pace of your speech is to suit the sense of what you are saying and make the audience respond to it in the right way.

Almost every great speech changes pace several times.

Almost every great speech changes pace several times. It is slow when the speaker wants his or her audience to stop and think (or laugh, cry or rage), and fast when he or she wants them to hurry on to the next point or to the conclusion.

Even a very short speech will have changes of pace. Read Lincoln's Gettysburg address again, all 269 words of it. After the stately, Biblical opening of 'Four score and seven years' the rest of the first sentence hurries on to its conclusion. Lincoln wanted his audience to agree quickly to his starting proposition. It contains a statement which was highly contentious in its time 'all men are created equal' and he did not want them to stop and think about it. But then he deliberately slows the second sentence down with two enforced pauses, before and after the words between the dashes. Having got the audience to accept quickly that the United States was founded in liberty and equality, Lincoln wants them to think in earnest whether it can endure.

We have already noticed, in passing, some techniques which great speakers have used to slow things down, as when Churchill uses the elaborate word 'subjugated'. John Donne, even more elaborately, uses Latin 'panem quotidianum' before translating it as 'daily bread': he stops his listeners cold and then makes them listen again to a key concept. Here are some other common devices which make a speech travel faster or slower.

For acceleration, you might try repeating a short phrase ('we shall fight them on the . . .'). Without repeating the same phrase, you can achieve the same effect by repeating the same construction. Here is Churchill again, attacking the Munich settlement in 1938:

> **"There can never be friendship between the British democracy and the Nazi power – that power which spurns Christian ethics, which cheers its onward course by a barbarous paganism, which vaunts the spirit of aggression and conquest, which derives strength and perverted pleasure from persecution, and uses – as we have seen – with pitiless brutality the threat of murderous force."**

That passage also contains two other familiar devices for acceleration. There is an alliteration (repeating words with the same initial letter) 'perverted pleasure from persecution'. Churchill also uses a matching construction. Instead of actually repeating a construction 'which . . . which . . . which . . .' he uses a matching construction in a way which gives equal weight to the two things which are matched together: 'uses – with *pitiless brutality* the threat of *murderous force*'. (This latter one is characteristically Churchillian: use it with caution if you want to avoid sounding like an inferior copy.)

In the John Donne passage, notice how much momentum he builds up with the use of repeated pairs of adjectives ('wintered and frozen, clouded and eclipsed, damped and benumbed, smothered and stupefied') until the five words which stop the listeners dead. (We are going to say more about pairs and trios in the section called 'Pairs and trios'.) In the context of pace, pairs tend to speed things up. Trios, words organized in groups of three, have great pace when the trio belong naturally together ('government of the people, by the people, for the people') but they stop a speech short when the third member is a deliberate surprise: 'in the same accident he managed to break his arm, his leg and his promise'.

One of the simplest ways to accelerate a speech is to begin sentences with connecting words. 'But . . . moreover . . . However . . . In other words . . . This means that . . .' And in speech, it is perfectly all right to begin a sentence with 'And . . .'

To slow a speech down, you can simply create pauses. A new paragraph, full stop, a colon, a dash or a parenthesis entail a pause. But this is not necessarily true of a question mark (see below on rhetorical questions). As we have seen, you can use unusual words and constructions to slow a speech down. But even more effectively, you can use a series of strong one-syllable words: 'now God comes to thee'. There is an analogy here with songwriting. A one-syllable rhyme (moon/June) is known as a masculine rhyme and a multi-syllable rhyme (greenery/scenery) is a feminine rhyme. Feminine rhymes are often favoured for fast, witty, patter songs, masculine rhymes are usually preferred in slow, romantic ballads.

It is a common mistake to imagine that short sentences accelerate a speech. A sentence always ends in a pause and the more pauses you have the more slowly you will speak. Ultra-short sentences bring a speech virtually to a halt. Especially a whole string of them. With no main verbs. If it is properly constructed, if words are grouped logically around ideas, if rhetorical devices are deployed in an exciting but appropriate way, a long sentence can have far more momentum than a short one.

To slow a speech down, you can simply create pauses.

Sometimes the same device can be used to speed things up or slow things down. A vivid metaphor or simile speeds things up if it is instantly comprehensible ('float like a butterfly, sting like a bee') and slows things down if the audience needs to think about it ('my opponent floats like a bee and stings like a butterfly'). A question slows things right down if you want the audience to answer it in their minds or directly from the floor ('how many people here have been victims of a crime in the last year?'). But you may ask what is called a rhetorical question, which you intend to answer yourself: 'why do the crime figures always lie?' In that case, you should ask and answer it quickly, before someone in the audience supplies the wrong answer.

Statistics are another weapon you can use either way. A string of simple statistics builds a great deal of pace if they all point to the same basic conclusion. An example might be: 'Small businesses in Oblivia – with less than 50 employees – employ nearly two-thirds of the nation's workers. Just over a quarter of all Oblivian workers are either self-employed or work for businesses with less than 10 people. Small businesses accounted for 68 per cent of the growth in GDP over the last five years, and for no less than 86 per cent of the new jobs created. In Oblivia today a new business is formed every five minutes . . .' (The figures all tell you that small businesses are really important in Oblivia.)

But a quirky statistic slows a speech down, as does a string of statistics with an unusual conclusion. An example might be: 'Last year the average Oblivian family spent $50 on charity appeals for victims of starvation, $747 on appeals from religious evangelists, and $2,142 on guns and ammunition.'

If you want your audience to agree something quickly, especially something contentious, express it quickly and simply as an accomplished fact.

If you want them to ponder something, express it slowly in a more complex way, with more exotic words and information, perhaps asking deliberate questions. You may even deliberately mystify your audience, and leave them to guess where you are taking them. This can build suspense and grab attention, but do not keep the mystery going for too long.

Finally, humour can be either speedy or slow. For speed, you tell a string of one-liners. To slow things down, you tell a story.

Fingers of speech

In this section we are going to look at a number of recognized figures of speech. Two of them are built into its title: 'fingers of speech' is a metaphor and a pun. If it did its job properly, it made you smile and it made you think. People often use their fingers to make a point, sometimes very directly and without the aid of speech. Young children use their fingers to paint with. Think of this next series of devices as something you can use to point or to paint. We will look at their strengths and their hazards.

Alliteration

Using repeated words or syllables with the same letter or sound, usually a consonant: 'An Austrian army awfully arrayed. Boldly by battery besieges Belgrade.' This is a stock device of great orators: we have seen one from Churchill ('perverted pleasure from persecution') and I heard a good modern example recently from an opponent of Tony Blair who accused the Prime Minister of allowing his critics to be 'exposed to the spite and spleen of his spin doctors'. Alliteration gives pace and emphasis (in the modern example the repeated sp- sound carries a special venom) and a short alliteration often sticks in the memory, particularly those beginning with the letter L (limousine liberal, lounge lizard, lager lout). However, at its worst alliteration sounds stilted and over-blown, as in the early 1970s when Vice-President Spiro T. Agnew perpetrated 'nattering nabobs of negativism' to attack the American media.

Anacoluthon

Deliberately changing the grammar of a sentence: this can be very effective after a long list, when the sudden change can wake an audience from a hypnotic trance. Although they do not come from a speech, there are some particularly effective examples in the Bible: 'The rest of all the acts of Asa, and all his might, and all that he did, and the cities which he built, are they not written in the book of the chronicles of the kings of Judah?' (King James Version 1 Kings 15:23). This is followed by a superb *bathos* (anti-climax): 'Nevertheless in the time of his old age he was diseased in his feet.' The danger of anacoluthon is that people may not recognize it as deliberate. They may simply think you have lost your way in a sentence. The following anacoluthon by George Bush senior, explaining his position on abortion, was probably unintentional:

"Well, it appears to a double standard to some, but I – that's my position, and it's – we don't have the time to philosophically discuss it here, but . . . we're going to opt on the side of life."

Anaphora

Repeating a word or phrase at the beginning of successive sentences ('we shall fight them on the . . .') and its companion *antistrophe*, repeating it at the end: Franklin Roosevelt used this device when he announced Pearl Harbor to the American people:

"In 1931, ten years ago, Japan invaded Manchukuo – without warning. In 1935, Italy invaded Ethiopia – without warning. In 1938, Hitler

occupied Austria – without warning. In 1939, Hitler invaded Czecho-slovakia – without warning. Later in 1939, Hitler invaded Poland – without warning. And now Japan has attacked Malaya and Thailand – and the United States – without warning.**"**

Both devices give speeches a strong sense of rhythm and they make ideas lodge in listeners' minds. Roosevelt did this so successfully that no one noticed that several of his examples were wrong.

Antithesis

Presenting contrasting ideas in an identical construction: 'The more I know men, the more I like dogs.' A simple device which makes a contrast more memorable.

Climax

Building words, phrases or ideas in sequence from those of least to those of greatest power: 'I do not like him, I do not trust him, I do not respect him, he is a liar, and a traitor, and an evil-doer.' Every speech should have a climax but only one, at the end of your speech. Its opposite number *bathos* usually creates laughter, usually accidentally, sometimes intentionally. 'I do not trust him, I do not respect him, he is a liar and a traitor and an evil-doer and I do not even like him.'

Euphemism

Using a softer substitute for a word with unpleasant associations, such as 'passed away' for 'died'. They have become particularly prevalent among military people, who used to be famous for speaking plainly, so that 'civilian casualties' have become 'collateral damage'. The modern age has produced a series of sickly euphemisms for mass murder and genocide. Political correctness has added a new crop of euphemisms (such as 'alternatively cerebral' for 'stupid') to protect selected groups of people (and animals, plants and even non-living things) from the associations of everyday speech. In general, avoid euphemism. At best it makes you sound mealy-mouthed, at worst, dishonest. However, for certain audiences a euphemism has become established and not using it carries a risk of deliberate discourtesy. For example, it is now a mistake to talk about 'old' or 'elderly' people.

In general, avoid euphemism. The polite term is 'older people'. However you may well exploit euphemisms for *irony* (see below): 'the village was targeted for close air support' (i.e. bombed) 'and a number of pre-adult civilian personnel were collaterally damaged' (children were killed).

Hyperbole

Exaggeration: President Nixon used it sincerely, if questionably, when the astronauts first landed on the moon: 'This is the greatest week in the history of the world since the creation.' Because of its associations with the lower reaches of advertising, PR and media, most speakers now use hyperbole ironically, to mock their opponents or, more rarely, themselves: 'The minister will be delighted to know that his statement on agricultural waste has caused dancing in the streets of my constituency. Grown men embraced each other and wept openly. Old people gazed at each other in disbelief that such a day had come at last.'

Irony

A statement which superficially means one thing but in fact conveys the exact opposite meaning to those who truly understand it: 'and Brutus was an honourable man'. When you use irony it is as if you were saying 'Not!' or 'Yeah right' to your audience. Irony is a marvellous

Irony is a marvellous but dangerous weapon. but dangerous weapon. At its best it demolishes your opponent's position, and in debate it may actually provoke your opponent into a foolish outburst. It can make your audience laugh and it flatters them by thinking them smart enough to understand your hidden meaning. But irony has three allied dangers. First, it depends on your ability (or your speaker's ability) to convey the hidden meaning by vocal mannerism. If you (or he or she) cannot manage this, do not attempt irony or write it into your speaker's remarks. Second, in spite of your best vocal efforts, or your speaker's, the audience may simply not detect the hidden meaning. This is especially true of audience members who are unfamiliar with English, for irony is a distinctly English style. Third, irony is often hard to detect in print. The printed form of your speech will not convey your mannerisms (adopted boring, sing-song voice with mocking smile). The reader could take it at face value. Read the extract of the speech by Dr Tony Wright MP at the end of this book. Are you certain that he did not mean it?

Meiosis

The opposite of hyperbole, deliberate understatement. The most famous meiosis in history was said by Emperor Hirohito of Japan, broadcasting the news of the atom bombs at Hiroshima and Nagasaki: 'the situation has developed, not necessarily to our advantage'. In a less grim context, meiosis is frequently used for ironic effect, particularly by English people: 'Rummaging in my attic the other day, I found a first folio edition of Shakespeare. Which was nice.'

Metaphor and simile

We have already encountered these when discussing analogy. They are essentially ways of comparing things which are unlike in order to bring out their surprising similarities. A simile does this job with linking words (like . . . as if . . .), a metaphor does it by identifying the two things directly. A great many jokes are built on similes ('why is a . . . like a . . . ?') and you can often use this technique yourself to good effect if you can find an exotic comparison and then explain it. But remember, as we said earlier, that metaphors and similes work when they make a fair and logical comparison. They can then combine an unforgettable image and an unforgettable idea. They do not work at all when they depend on words alone, and they will invariably puzzle and annoy your audience. A few general tips on metaphors and similes:

1. Many metaphors are delivered effectively in the form 'A is the X of Y' as in 'He is the Homer Simpson of British politics'.

2. You can often work an effective switch on a simple metaphor or simile 'he is like Homer Simpson, without the brains', although this technique is teetering on the edge of cliché.

3. A metaphor or simile can be as long or as short as you like. In old times, writers and speakers used to employ long, sustained metaphors. Read the dedication of the King James Bible with its long image of the king as a new sun dispelling the dark clouds which had formed after the extinction of the star of Queen Elizabeth. My former boss, Denis Healey, revived the technique to good effect with a sustained comparison of Margaret Thatcher and John Major to Lucy and Charlie Brown (see Appendix). By sustaining the metaphor, he made his listeners locate his political opponents in a cartoon world.

    If you do use a sustained simile or metaphor, make sure that its comparisons remain consistently logical. Margaret Thatcher and John Major really were like Lucy and Charlie Brown.

4. Metaphors and similes often hunt well in pairs: 'In the criminal underworld of disease, bacteria are muggers and viruses are squatters. Bacteria knock you down openly in the street, viruses sneak into your house and take it over.'

5. Mixed metaphors are usually funny by accident. Britain's post-war Foreign Secretary, Ernest Bevin, produced a spectacular example: 'If you open up that Pandora's Box you don't know what Trojan horses might come jumping out.' If you are very daring you might want to achieve this effect deliberately: 'the President is playing cocktail piano in the depths of an ocean of sleaze' but as with irony you had better be sure that your audience will get it.

6. A good metaphor does not always have to use an everyday image. One of the greatest and enduring metaphors 'Iron Curtain' is a weird image. But it is easy to imagine and it was superbly logical in its context.

Iron Curtain is unusual in having such a long and active life. Most metaphors do not survive their initial flight. Others turn into zombies – the living dead – in the twilight zone of cliché. 'Political football' must have been fresh once as were its companions 'level playing field' and 'moving the goalposts'. You can have a lot of fun with clichés, by deliberately sustaining them or by running them together: 'The government has treated the Health Service as a political football but it keeps moving the goalposts for health service managers. There is no level playing field between health authorities and it is no wonder that no one listens to the minister when he blows the whistle as a referee.'

Some almost dead metaphors twitch into life in the wrong company. 'A grass roots initiative' is a clichéd way of describing any idea which springs from people (cliché alert) 'on the ground'. It is usually a harmless thing to say, but when a British minister called for 'grass roots initiatives to transform our urban parks and green spaces' it produced an unexpected image of planting new lawns.

Oxymoron and paradox

Paradox is saying something apparently illogical but which in fact makes sense. Groucho Marx's remark 'I don't want to belong to any club that would have me as a member' is an example. An oxymoron is specialized paradox – putting two apparently contradictory words together 'inspired stupidity', 'exquisite torture'. Many speakers now get a cheap joke out of explaining the term: 'it's an oxymoron, like *deeply shallow* or *military intelligence*' but this is becoming passionately boring. Paradox works if it is instantly understandable, like Groucho Marx's. If you need to explain a paradox, put the explanation *before* you deliver the paradox. Here's an example: 'Gordon Brown relies on the Treasury forecast of the economy. The Treasury forecast looks at no fewer than 357 economic variables, things that can affect the economy. So it has 357 things which can go wrong. Compare this to a horse. A horse has just four legs which can go wrong. So it would be far safer for Gordon Brown to bet all the nation's money on a horse.'

Pleonasm and tautology

Pleonasm means deliberately using extra words which add nothing to a concept: 'Well I have never seen anything like that in all my born days.' Tautology means saying the same thing twice or more in different words 'do not despair, be of good cheer'. These devices were used regularly in the past to give rhythm to speeches and emphasis to key ideas. Today they are becoming gifts for satirists: 'the past is behind us, the future lies ahead'. I would like to exchange words with the speech-writer who persuaded Vice-President Dan Quayle to say 'if we don't succeed, we run the risk of failure'.

Puns

Using a word, or a sound, with two different meanings at the same time or in the same context, to produce an unexpected or amusing effect. ('My lizard keeps telling jokes. *Your lizard keeps telling jokes?* Yes, he's a stand-up chameleon.') Any pun is a high-risk strategy. It is another very English form of humour and many of your audience may not get it if they are not well-versed in the English language. Even if they do get it,

Any pun is a high-risk strategy.

many will affect to despise puns and will groan ostentatiously: be prepared for this or your timing will suffer. For that reason, puns often work best in rapid clusters, so that each one 'tops' the previous one and does not allow the audience to dwell on it. This was a good cluster, in an entertaining speech about bad gardening. 'In my garden a fuschia has no future, a clematis becomes a clemortis, a nasturtium becomes a nasty urtium, a begonia is a begonner, and an aster turns into a disaster.' Puns should not be laboured – if you cannot work them naturally and seamlessly into a single sentence, discard them. Like all jokes and humour, a pun should be relevant, not a piece of incidental entertainment.

Rhetorical question

Asking a question which the speaker intends to answer immediately in his or her own words. It can be a very effective device, particularly if you want to shut down other replies to an open-ended and contentious question. The big risk is that someone will answer it before you do. British Prime Minister Harold Wilson was discomfited many years ago in a campaign appearance in a naval town when he asked, 'Why do I stress the importance of the navy?' and someone shouted out, 'Because you're in Chatham!'

Numbers are metaphors

Many years ago at college I used to read *China Pictorial*, the colour magazine which was sent to us free by Chairman Mao's government. It always contained fascinating detailed statistics. 'In the anti-pest campaign in Fukien province, guided by Mao Tse-Tung thought, 5,617,987 bugs were eradicated.' I always wondered if someone counted each individual bug. Instead I was told at the time that the Chinese treated numbers as metaphors, not necessarily literally true but denoting a lot or a little. The more precise the number, the more important it was.

Although it is still important to get numbers right, there is something to be learnt from those copies of *China Pictorial*. There is no point in using a number at all, unless it conveys an impression of magnitude. We have already discussed in Chapter 7 some techniques for making numbers relevant to an audience, such as dividing big numbers into smaller familiar ones and finding sensible comparators.

China Pictorial was right to use very precise numbers. They do make people think. It is very easy to do this yourself, especially if you link the very precise number to something that cannot be precise or even measured at all: 'It is a scientific fact that 86.74 per cent of all males over 15 need at least five minutes to put a duvet cover back onto a duvet.' (Incidentally, the words 'it is a scientific fact' in a speech nearly always mean the complete opposite.) When you are talking about the time of some future event, it is often very effective to identify it precisely. Compare 'at this rate of destruction the Amazon rain forest will have disappeared by 2030' to 'at this rate, the last tree in the Amazon will be cut down on 5 July 2029, at 5.37 pm local time.'

Pairs and trios

At the risk of seeming obsessive, I recommend yet again that you keep alert in your speech for opportunities to use pairs and trios.

We have already seen examples of what they can achieve in the right hands. Pairs of words can give your speech music, pairs of ideas lend themselves naturally to contrast and comparison. Both these effects can be found in the same sentence of the Gettysburg address: 'The world will little note nor long remember what we say here, but it can never forget what they did here.'

A trio – ideas organized in clusters of three – can give your speech tremendous momentum. A trio automatically conveys a sense of progress. You can use it to build a crescendo from a to B to **C** ('I came, I saw, I conquered') or equally to achieve surprise by going from a to B to **D** ('I came, I saw, I went home').

As we have seen earlier, groups of three are the easiest number for an audience to remember. St Paul knew that when he said 'Now there abideth three things: faith, hope and charity.' The world's armies know that when they issue orders in threes: 'Ready, aim, fire!' Three is the ideal number for any list. If you must have more than three items on a list, make it five not four because any odd number is more memorable than any even number. Seven is definitely too many for a list (try remembering instantly each one of the Seven Dwarfs).

Stop me if you have heard this before

Humour is a terrible risk in any speech. It takes a professional comedian years of training and a million cold audiences ('you could have stored meat in them') to learn to make people laugh. Why should you be able to do it as an amateur?

Humour is a terrible risk in any speech. No speech actually needs humour. Even a speech intended for entertainment does not have to be humorous: you can entertain people by being interesting – and interested in them – far better than telling a string of jokes, however hilarious. Many sports personalities try to convert themselves into comedians when they go on the after-dinner speaking circuit. A few succeed very well, but the rest would do better to say what it is really like to be a professional sportsperson, or better still, give a masterclass.

If you must be a humorist, at least avoid making mistakes. The biggest mistake is irrelevance. Humour works when it is integrated into your speech, making the points you want remembered, not when it is poured in from outside in the hope of making it more entertaining. Humour should be part of the hamburger, not the ketchup.

The second biggest mistake is offence. It is no good grumbling about political correctness, but you really cannot make a joke in any audience about race, disability, religion, gender, age, sexual orientation, nationality, illness or size. A British politician recently lost her job for a joke about race in what she thought was a 'safe' audience, and rightly so. There are no safe audiences any more, and even if there were it has become bad manners and a sign of a limited mind to make a joke at any formal occasion which uses these aspects of human life in a stereotyped way. Is that how you want to be remembered? It is equally wrong to tell jokes which rely on bad language or references to sex, drug abuse (including alcohol) and 'rude' bodily functions, especially the elimination of any form of waste. Although they may not be obviously offensive, it is foolish to tell any jokes which rely on a special accent or mannerism. It is also wise to avoid any jokes about contemporary politics, and any jokes against a current celebrity (you do not know how many fans he or she has in the audience). As you can see, there are not many jokes left.

The third mistake is to tell jokes against your audience. Most speakers have enough sense to avoid insulting their audience collectively. But it is quite easy to insult a group by insulting one member of it. If you are talking to a convention of dentists, do not tell any story, however fascinating or hilarious, about any current dentist, however far away from this particular convention. Your joke dentist is still a fellow professional to them. It is far better to tell a funny story about a dentist *in history* – which makes no judgement on the profession now and by implication, compliments the audience for their advances in dentistry.

A more common mistake is to tell too many stories against yourself. You are their distinguished guest speaker – do not leave them to remember you as a klutz.

Do not tell esoteric jokes or stories, which force an audience to know too much or to understand too much fine English. It is extraordinarily difficult to judge what references any audience can be expected to understand without explanation. In the 1930s it was commonplace for British politicians to quote Dickens. They could expect to be understood, because thousands of homes had complete sets of Dickens, given away in the newspaper circulation wars of the time. Newspapers do not use that form of promotion today, and British politicians will now talk about sport or television rather than Dickens.

However, if for some reason you want to make a very obscure reference you may obtain a humorous and flattering effect by assuming that your audience knows it already, as it might be: 'We all remember the wise words of the seventeenth-century Swedish Chancellor Oxenstjerna . . .'

A much worse mistake than being esoteric is to tell any joke or story in which you have to pretend to be a member of the same group as the audience. It will simply show how clearly you are not.

I dislike hearing quotations of any kind in speeches. Humorous quotations can leaden the lightest speech, and people have usually heard them already. I dislike hearing quotations of any kind in speeches; all quotations, however brilliant, are second-hand words and second-hand thoughts. However, you can sometimes achieve an entertaining effect by using quotations indirectly in a throwaway style: 'The goal made a big difference to the team. All the players stiffened their sinews and some even summoned up the blood.'

You can often get more humour from a weird fact or story, or even a single weird sentence than from a setpiece joke or story. (One of my favourites is the weird but commonplace sign which says 'Dogs must be led beyond this point.' I imagine hordes of puzzled pedestrians looking desperately for a dog to lead beyond the point. I also enjoy 'This door is alarmed' – so what, I'm terrified.)

A joke or story dies as soon as a speaker says 'That reminds me of the story . . .' Humour in a speech should be like an expensive hairpiece, and no one should see the join.

In my view, any one-liner is always better than any long story. It takes less time, it is easier to slide it in, and, above all, you are less likely to forget it or to stumble over some vital element in the build-up.

In terms of actual delivery, a common mistake in telling a joke or story is not to pause for a laugh. An even commoner mistake is pausing for a laugh when there is clearly not going to be one.

The biggest mistake of all is to comment in any way on the absence of a laugh.

SUMMARY

- A speech needs colour, rhythm, pace, emotion – and variety.

- There are many tricks and techniques to achieve colour and variety. Test them by ear. Some you can also test by eye: the length of sentences and paragraphs on the page.

- Simple words in logical groups can generate a natural rhythm. Keep subjects and verbs close together.

- Great speeches have changes of pace. You can achieve this through both sound and sense.

- Speed your speech up when you want your audience to accept something quickly. Slow it down when you want them to think.

- Sometimes the same technique (metaphor, statistics, humour, trios) can be used as an accelerator or as a brake.

- There are well-established figures of speech which can be used to add colour, and make a point more memorable. Some are dangerous – especially irony.

- Metaphors and similes are immensely varied and flexible, but they should always be logical. Metaphors can turn all too quickly into clichés.

- Numbers have a role as metaphors. When you use them, be certain that they mean 'something big' or 'something small' to your audience.

- Pairs of words or phrases can give a speech music and bring home a contrast or comparison.

- Trios – ideas in clusters of three – are especially easy to remember. They can build momentum, crescendo or surprise.

- Humour is a high risk. Make humour relevant and understandable, and slide it easily into your speech. Do not cause offence. Short passages of humour usually work better than long stories.

- Be prepared for humour to fail.

9

Tricks and techniques: perswaysion

How to win over neutrals, doubters and enemies

In this chapter we are going to look at certain techniques for winning over a neutral, doubtful or hostile audience. As before, you have probably used them already, hundreds of times. Some of them are historic forms of logical argument or long-established means of persuasion, but for a modern audience it is become dangerous to argue, and almost as dangerous to persuade.

Arguing is out of style. For thousands of years, from the ancient Greeks until the 1920s it was a major form of public entertainment. People went to debates and public meetings to enjoy watching other people argue with each other and to join in the argument themselves. **Arguing is** They took sides and they wanted their side to win, crushingly. **out of style.** If they went to see a solo speaker, whether a preacher or a salesman, they expected him to battle for their hearts and their minds or their money.

What changed in the 1920s was radio. Through radio, people could go to meetings without leaving their living room. In the new setting, argument became not only old-fashioned but positively unpleasant. That effect was greatly magnified by television, so much so that arguers almost never win on television. They may have all the facts, all the logic on their side, but in someone's living room they seem strident and hectoring and generally not nice people. Television has rewarded politicians, and public speakers, who are measured rather than driven, who are plausible rather than overwhelming, who cajole rather than argue and because television is so pervasive people expect the same style from speakers in any setting.

People mentally spend their entire life in their living room, even at a public meeting. People do not like strangers to argue with them in their living room. So we will avoid the term 'argument'. They are usually suspicious of strangers who try to persuade them of something in their living room, because they associate this with high-pressure salesmanship. So we will also avoid the term 'persuasion'. Instead, for the sake of a pun, I invented the word 'perswaysion' – the art of swaying an audience without letting them know what you are doing to them.

In previous chapters, I have advised you to test your speech by talking it out as you compose it, and check whether it would sound right in conversation. That is especially important when you are trying the arts of perswaysion. Would you want to sound like that as a guest in someone's living room? No one likes a guest who domineers, or rants, or shouts and if your audience remembers you that way you have lost all the arguments before you even start. After you have won over the audience by all means work yourself up and work them up with you.

No one likes a guest who domineers, or rants, or shouts.

Know your audience

We have already talked a great deal about knowing your audience. It is basic good manners for any speech, and it is essential if you want to sway them.

You should be able to answer correctly *all* of these questions about your audience although as we shall see later on you should actually *avoid* using some of the answers:

1. Who would they accept as a hero and an authority – someone you could cite as being on your side?

2. Who would represent a villain or a clown to them – someone you could associate with the *other* side?

3. What kind of everyday analogy would they accept as logical and persuasive? What cultural, scientific, general knowledge could you cite in your support and expect them to understand?

4. What is the ground from which they draw their goals, their facts and their logic, where do arguments have to be located to make sense to them? Let me give an extreme example. You are speaking to a group of Christian fundamentalists in defence of the right to choose an abortion. I would not recommend you to accept such an engagement, but you have done. If you want to engage with this audience at all, let alone sway them, you must *begin* your reasoning at the same place as theirs. You cannot start from the rights of women, or the dangers of suffering and crime from making abortions unlawful, or the legal and constitutional guarantees which a ban on abortion would violate. With that particular audience the Bible is the source of all truth so you begin your arguments from the Bible, and what is more, the same translation as they use. (Hint: if you are in this situation, try starting from Matthew 22:21 and then construct the argument that the laws of God should not be enforced through the laws of man.)

5. Finally, and invariably, what benefit will your audience obtain from agreeing with you and doing what you want? You *must* be able to complete the sentence Vote for Me (or Buy my Product or Give me your Money or Sign the Petition) and . . . What follows 'and' must be something important to your audience.

I repeat, you must answer *all* the questions before you construct your appeal to the audience. At best the exercise will unlock your imagination and produce unexpected connections between what your audience wants and believes in and what you are offering them. (It will also give your audience the ammunition they need to sway other people who could not get to the meeting.) At worst, it will stop you losing your audience in the first minute.

Not long ago, I was a speaker at a meeting about the euro in an English country town. The previous speaker was a scholarly lord. He spoke for 15 minutes on why Shakespeare would have been against the euro. It was fascinating (although it was also a fine example of Irrelevant authority – see below) but it was lost on his audience. The earl gave himself no chance of swaying anybody in the room. He gave no one in the room any ammunition for swaying anybody who had not come to the meeting. He became purely an entertainer.

The exercise I have just described makes some speakers unhappy. They think that it represents 'dumbing down' or worse, dishonesty. In the Introduction, I said strongly: be true to yourself, and don't pretend to be part of the same group as your audience if you are not. But is that not exactly what the exercise will make you do?

I think not. First of all, I do not think it represents 'dumbing down' to cut out references which an audience will not understand in favour of those which they will. Dumbing down to me means artificially simplifying a subject and translating it spuriously into the world of mass culture. I once heard a history teacher tell his teenage students that Queen Elizabeth I was 'quite a babe'. It left them cold (teenagers do not like people who condescend and besides, 'babe' was already out of date as slang). But when he told them that she was 'broke', he got them interested. The class discussed the way she saved and borrowed money and stayed in her friends' houses without paying for her share of the food and expenses, and how these things compared with the way teenagers behaved. 'Babe' was fake and dumbing-down; 'broke' was honest and vivid.

Nor is the exercise meant to make you abandon your values or to conceal them. It is simply meant to make you understand your audience's values, so that you can choose a pathway for a logical journey. You may not agree with that pathway, but you can show that by making the right logical journey using that pathway you and they will get to your desired conclusion. Having got there together, you might then be able to show your audience how much easier the journey would have been if you had used another pathway.

That process is not intellectual treachery, but engagement with your audience. If you are not willing to find a common starting point with your audience, you might just as well shout at them 'Everything you believe in is stupid and it is time you saw things my way. Get real, you dummies!'

Common ground

Finding the common ground is an essential theme of any speech where you have to sway any audience. The common ground is what you and the audience both think is *right and reasonable*.

In most settings it is an easy task to find the common ground. If you do the fifth part of the exercise I described in the last section, about 90 per cent of the time you can complete the sentence Vote for Me . . . Buy my Product . . . Give me your Money . . . Sign the Petition . . . with the words 'and it will improve your well-being'. Occasionally you may have to vary the formula a little to say 'and it will improve the well-being of your family/neighbourhood/business/organization/cat'. The common ground is that it is *right and reasonable* for people to want to improve their personal circumstances and those of the people (or cats) in their near circle. Of course people do also look beyond their personal circle, and other possible common ground might be supporting our country, helping those less fortunate, saving the planet. More and more audiences today expect both, that is to improve their lives and salve their consciences: hence the growing sales of 'ethical' products and services. With this kind of audience you will have to widen the common ground to something like Vote for Me, etc. . . . and do yourself and the planet a favour.

Sometimes the common ground may be a general principle with a high degree of abstraction. For example, you and your audience might agree that it is *right and reasonable* to prevent cruelty, maintain the rule of law, promote equality, uphold democracy and the will of the people. If you are a long way from your audience intellectually, you may have to travel into a very high level of abstraction to find the common ground between you. In my extreme example (you pro-choice on abortion speaking to audience of fundamentalist Christians) the common ground would be at a very high peak of abstraction. It would be something like: it is *right and reasonable* that all laws should be based on general moral principles and not just for the convenience of society. From that lofty peak of abstraction there will be many different pathways down into the everyday real world, and each pathway will itself break up into many different turnings and by-ways. In my example, you chose a pathway you would normally reject because that audience simply would not take any other. But you still started the journey together, on common ground.

At other times, the common ground is very down to earth. In the United States I once saw a local politician campaign on the slogan 'Re-elect X to the state assembly, he's too old to go to work'. He and his audience agreed that it was *right and reasonable* that ageing politicians should not have to cope with a real job and he won by a landslide.

The hardest audience in which to find any common ground is of course children. In any discussion, almost any child can be guaranteed to query or reject any reason for doing or believing anything. This is partly genuine intellectual curiosity and partly because it is a safe way to drive any adult into a frenzy. The discussion will often end with the words 'Because I say so!', which, curiously enough, may be the common ground which the child actually wants, since most children think it *right and reasonable* to meet the request of an adult who cares for them. If you are speaking to children and are seeking to sway them as well as informing and entertaining them, it is worth giving up some of *your* speaking time to let *them* help to define the common ground. At least ask questions 'Who thinks it's a good idea to . . . ?' and wait for hands up.

With most adult audiences, you will not take up much time establishing the common ground. In fact, as we have already seen, the more time you spend on it, the more likely it is that your audience will think about it and the greater the risk that they might reject it.

The common ground, therefore, is where you start the intellectual journey of your perswaysive speech. You choose a pathway your audience is willing to follow and you show that it could not conceivably lead them anywhere else but to your destination.

For any audience, you always have competitors. Your problem is that there is always competition. For any audience, you always have competitors. In a formal debate you can actually see them and you know what strategy they are using. Otherwise you have to imagine them – the invisible enemy trying to conquer your audience's hearts and minds.

Essentially your competitors have two choices. They can either fight you for ownership of the same common ground with the audience, or they can suggest a different common ground to the audience. The first is the general practice in modern politics: almost every mainstream party promises to make people better off, and they then offer a journey which leads to the inescapable conclusion of voting for them. It is usually left to fringe parties and single-interest groups to try to change the common ground and offer the audience another starting point (as it might be, local independence, or the environment, or equality, or saving the neighbourhood school).

In the world outside politics, your competitors may use either strategy or indeed both at once. In business, your competitors might offer a better version of your product or service: Sudso Washes Whiter. That is fighting for your common ground. But they might offer your audience a different starting point: Sudso Saves the Planet. You might choose to fight back on your common ground: Albedo for Whiteness You Can Trust. They might fight on your ground and theirs: Sudso Washes Whiter – and Greener. You might then want to occupy another piece of common ground: Be an Albedo Mum.

Whether your competitors are visible or invisible, you must think about their strategy and how to counteract it.

In the world of charities and volunteering, the competition is nearly all on the second level, that is, arguing over the common ground rather than the subsequent journey. Most charities and voluntary groups invite their audience to make their cause their number one priority – it is less usual for them to say that they do a better job of helping that cause than their competitors.

Whether your competitors are visible, in a public debate, or invisible, you must think about their strategy and how to counteract it. If the enemy have accepted your common ground, you fight them on the subsequent journey. If they are challenging your chosen common ground, you must decide whether you are confident enough in your choice. If you are, you can ignore their chosen ground and again concentrate on the subsequent journey. If you are nervous that the enemy might have chosen a more attractive common ground, you could try bolstering your chosen ground by adding other attractive territory to it. 'Ladies and gentlemen, for centuries a white wash has been a sign of love and care for a family. And it was a great human achievement, a victory over a grimy, dirty world. Today, thanks to Albedo, it is so much easier to get a perfect white wash. But those values of love and care and the triumph of the human spirit, those are still Albedo's values today.' Alternatively, you might simply annex your opponents' territory: 'Ladies and gentlemen, of course we all want to save the planet. But that does not mean that we have to give up a perfect white wash . . .'

When you speak, you should know your audience and know your competitors. That should tell you how to fight them off.

Accentuate the positive

Whatever your intellectual competitors, positive arguments for your case are always better than negative arguments against theirs.

That is simple common sense. Disproving the opposition case does not prove yours. No audience likes being forced into a conclusion, being told 'You can either have A or B, and since A is clearly wrong, you are stuck with B.' Women especially resist that kind of linear logic. In any set of choices, it is always possible to imagine more, and if you knock down the opposition choice the audience might still prefer to search for their ideal choice rather than accept the one you give them.

Using negative arguments makes you sound negative, which for any audience is perilously close to being unpleasant.

Even if there is a totally closed set of choices and you wipe out all the other possible choices, you still may not win over your audience. Suppose, to give a silly example, you are in a debate about which is the best of the Seven Dwarfs. You could destroy the case for Bashful, Doc, Sneezy, Happy, Grumpy and Sleepy and still not persuade the audience to vote for Dopey. (The audience might be sick of all dwarfs without exception, especially if all the other champions have followed the same tactics of destroying the competition.)

There is another common-sense reason for accentuating the positive. Even if you destroy the opposition case, you do actually remind your audience that it exists. If they think that your destruction is in some way unfair you may actually reinforce their loyalty to the opposition.

Finally, of course, using negative arguments makes you sound negative, which for any audience is perilously close to being unpleasant. If you are not careful negative arguments can tempt you into being sarcastic and cutting – a fatal move.

There are two exceptions to the principle of avoiding negative arguments.

First, if you are defending a status quo with which your audience is reasonably happy, it is reasonable and productive to dwell on the risks of changing it. (This is particularly true with British audiences.) Talking about the risks of change is not quite the same as being negative, because at least by implication you are talking about the good things in the status quo.

Second, some part of the opposition case might so dominate the audience's thinking on an issue that you simply have to get rid of it before they will follow you anywhere. As we will see in the next sections, there are two honest ways in which you can do this and several dishonest ones.

Dealing with the opposition (honestly)

Whatever side you take in an argument, it would be very unusual if your opposition had no case at all. They would have to be completely evil or completely stupid. In a formal debate you simply will not get opponents of that quality: if the organizer of the debate had the sense to invite *you* he or she will probably have the sense to invite opponents who are reasonably competent and honest. But if you are speaking solo and imagining your invisible opponents it would be foolish to think of them all as evil or stupid. If they were, they would not have any appeal to your audience.

The first principle of dealing with your opposition is respect, and from respect flows honesty.

If the opposition (real or invisible) has some good points on their side, you should admit them. You should then try to reduce their impact immediately and suggest to the audience that they are far less significant than some big points of your own. Two examples come to mind, on either side of the euro debate in Britain.

If you were *for* joining the euro, you might concede that this would mean Britain giving up control of her exchange rate and her interest rates. But you might then immediately suggest that Britain has little real control over her exchange rate and her interest rates – they are set by outside market forces. The economic benefit of clinging to that very nominal control of interest rates and the exchange rate would be far less than the economic gains of being a full member of the biggest single market in the world.

If you were *against* joining the euro, you might concede that joining would remove the risk of loss to British business from foreign exchange movements when it trades with the other euro countries. But you would then immediately suggest that the risk would still be there for trade with the United States and anywhere outside the euro and that the gains from eliminating foreign exchange risks would be far smaller than the risk to British business of Britain being trapped in the wrong exchange rate or the wrong interest rate. (In both cases the common ground with the audience is the same: it is *right and reasonable* to make the British economy stronger.)

If you adopt this strategy you not only eliminate your opponent's good point but you make the audience like and respect you for being fair-minded – a big gain in any setting.

However, if your opponent's main point against you is wrong, you must demonstrate this honestly, and refute it with one or more 'killer facts'.

Using the killer fact

A killer fact is (a) true; (b) from a trusted source; (c) devastating to the opposing case. Once it is admitted, its logic points to only one conclusion, that your opponents are wrong and if they persist in their case they will prove that they are irrational, prejudiced and unreliable.

Killer facts can come as single shots or as salvoes. Suppose, for example, you had to deal with an opposition claim that 'immigrants are a drain on the British economy'. A killer fact would be: 'According to the National Statistical Office immigrants to Britain contributed 10 per cent of our national output last year.' Following the principle of making numbers comprehensible you would quickly add: 'That means they contributed around £1,600 to every man, woman and child in this country.' To build that into a salvo you might add: 'Immigrants actually contributed seven times more to our economy than North Sea oil.' To fire another shot you could also add: 'Immigrants also pay in more taxes to Treasury than they take out in benefits. Last year they paid in £2.6 billion more than they took out – that is worth over a penny on the standard rate of income tax.' At the end of that salvo, your audience might choose not to believe the facts (although they will have no reason to do this) but if they do accept the facts they cannot escape the conclusion that immigrants are *not* a drain on the economy. (Incidentally, all the facts in this cluster are true. All the other 'facts' in my examples are made up, to illustrate a point about writing, but the cluster in this paragraph is truth as well as an illustration.)

Killer facts can come as single shots or as salvoes.

With a neutral or unfriendly audience, you use your killer fact in a direct and prominent way. You warn the audience that it is coming and that you want them to listen to it. You might say 'My opponents said/you often hear X. That is wrong. The facts tell a different story. The facts are . . . So far from X, the fact is not-X.' (It is well worth repeating the word 'fact'. It inspires respect. 'The facts show' is a better thing to say than 'statistics show' or 'science shows' and is a league ahead of 'experts have proved'.)

However, with a friendly audience you may get a bigger effect from your killer fact by sliding it in unobtrusively so that they suddenly realize that it hit them. This is especially true when your killer fact is challenging the conventional wisdom of the audience. There is a good example of this in the speech by Sir David Ramsbotham in the Appendix – so good that I am going to challenge you to find it.

As we have said, a fact becomes a killer when its conclusion is inescapable. Scientists are always hunting for them, and one could even say that scientific theory has evolved precisely to turn facts into killers: the solution turned red, it *must* be an acid. It is hard to find facts which are that good, and you may just have to fall back on a wounding fact, one which damages the opposing case without making it untenable. A good example of a wounding fact is when you offer a single counter-example to a general proposition by the opposing camp. Suppose you had to combat the idea that 'women can never be strong national leaders'. You might riposte immediately 'Margaret Thatcher'. In formal logic that is a killer fact (it actually disproves the universal statement) but in everyday life it is no more than wounding. An opponent can still claim that she is an 'exception' (possibly even the mythical exception that 'proves the rule'). If you throw in more counter-examples, say Indira Gandhi, Golda Meir, the Dragon-Empress of China, Catherine the Great, Elizabeth I, Joan of Arc, the wounds get deeper and deeper and probably terminal.

Whether killing or wounding, your facts must be used honestly.

Whether killing or wounding, your facts must be used honestly. They must be relevant and they must address your opponent's real position, not a version of that position which you have invented for yourself. This is called Fighting the Man of Straw and it is one of the commonest forms of dishonest argument.

Killer logic

Sometimes you may not have a killer fact to eliminate an opposing argument. You simply may not know enough, or the opposing point may be too vague and general to be debated in terms of fact. In that case, you will have to fall back on killer logic. Unfortunately, logic is not nearly so reliable an assassin.

In killer logic you try to demonstrate, honestly, the gruesome consequences of your opponent's position, and force them to admit them. However, your opponents can wriggle hard against the admission – very often they will say 'That's different!' Or they may be robust enough to admit all of your consequences and still stick to their position.

Take the example of a debate on controlling traffic in cities. You are in favour. The opponents might argue that it is wrong in principle to restrict the right of people to move in public places and choose their form of transport. Very well, you riposte, so you are quite prepared to accept any number and any kind of vehicles in cities, and you are prepared to accept *all* the congestion, pollution, accidents, ill-health, economic loss they might cause. The opponents are entitled to say yes, they are: personal liberty is more important than any of these things. You have not killed them, but at least your logic has forced them into the admission and showed the audience where they stand.

One aspect of killer logic is worth remembering. If you are on the side of any kind of change there is *always* an opposing position to yours – doing nothing and maintaining the status quo. Somewhere in your speech you must convince the audience that the status quo is wrong and unacceptable. Obviously the best way to do this is to make its wrongness part of the common ground between you and them.

Dealing with your opponents (dubiously)

In this section we are going to look at a collection of debating tricks which you have almost certainly heard both in formal debate and in everyday life. Some are actually fallacies – *bad* arguments which no one should use. Others can be used honestly, but are usually not. I do not want to encourage you to use any of these debating tricks – although they do often work – but I hope the list will help you recognize them and riposte to them when the enemy uses them against you.

Ad hominem arguments

Attacking the personality or personalities on the opposite side rather than their arguments: this is always irrelevant and when your opponents are in the same room it is also bad-mannered and your host and your audience will not like it. It is a special mistake to use arguments ad hominem when your opponent is a feminam.

It is a special mistake to use arguments ad hominem when your opponent is a feminam.

It is terribly tempting to go for your opponent if he has been inconsistent or outrightly dishonest about an issue. Politicians regularly fall into this temptation. They employ armies of researchers to look up their opponents' records and parade their contradictions and broken promises. It is a complete waste of effort. No one could care less about any politician's record. Remember this story of Huey Long, the charismatic, dangerous governor of Louisiana in the 1930s. He was up for re-election and had to revisit a small town on the Mississippi river. On his first campaign he had promised them a new bridge. Not one foot of the bridge had been built, nor any plan made or even a sketch. His aides were in a panic: how would the governor explain away the broken promise? Long answered 'Tell them I lied.' The town voted him back with a large majority.

It is equally tempting to bait a live opponent if you know he is likely to lose his temper. Again resist the temptation. No audience likes a display of bad temper (especially an English audience) and they tend to blame equally everybody who was on the scene. Some of the audience will spot that you baited your opponent and will mark you down as a nasty little stirrer.

Do not attack your opponents personally. Attack what they say and do. (See also 'Guilt By association'.)

Begging the question

Building an argument on an assumption which you have yet to prove: 'The question is simple: what trust can you put in a man with an unbroken record of broken promises?' Did he in fact break his promises? Prove it.

Circular argument

A fallacy closely allied to begging the question: using two unproven assertions to support each other. 'My client is honest and upright. He belongs to the Loan Sharks Association, which admits only members who are honest and upright, and last year he was elected to its Ethics Committee.' Prove that your client is honest and upright: prove that the Association has that admissions policy.

Common foe

A very common device: the speaker identifies a common foe for himself or herself and the audience and then assumes that since they are united against the common foe they must be united on everything. The first half of this may well be correct and it may be a legitimate way of defining the common ground. But the second half of the common foe argument is wrong, as is the implication that any opponents of the speaker must be on the side of the common foe. Most speakers choose someone or something specific and detested as the common foe, but it is often more effective if the common foe is more amorphous and shadowy. Tony Blair used the technique brilliantly a few years ago when he united his somewhat discontented Labour party against 'the forces of conservatism' whom he blamed for no less than 17 bad things, from terrorism to snobbery.

False analogy

We have discussed earlier why analogies need to be honest. False analogies are a common device for misleading audiences and trapping or labelling opponents. A historic false analogy was the trick question put to conscientious objectors in World War One: 'What would you do if you saw a German raping your sister?' It is a false analogy because people do not have to judge the case for war against the whole German nation in the same terms as they judge an evil act by one hypothetical German.

False choice

Narrowing the choices for an audience so that the only alternative to the speaker's choice is something clearly wrong or unpopular: 'Let me be quite clear: the alternative to bombing Saddam Hussein is to do nothing about Saddam Hussein, to let him oppress and torture his own people and let him build up an arsenal of weapons of mass destruction.'

False connections

Assuming that two or more facts are connected, especially that one fact is the cause of another, when there is no evidence for this. P. G. Wodehouse's Uncle Galahad commits this fallacy when he explains why he drinks whisky: 'I knew a chap who gave up whisky and three days later he was knocked over by a cab.' It is also regularly used in debates on crime, both by liberals who link rising crime to unemployment and conservatives who link it to soft sentences by judges.

False inference

Using statistics or facts to 'prove' something which they do not: an example would be quoting the (hypothetical) statistic that 90 per cent of all heroin users began by experimenting with cannabis, in order to support a continued prohibition on cannabis. There may be reasons for banning cannabis but this is not one of them. For all we know, the same 90 per cent began by experimenting with alcohol or banana skins or dissolving aspirin in Coca-Cola. The mirror-image statistic would be legitimate and impressive – if 90 per cent of all cannabis users went on to heroin – but only if it were true.

Guilt by association

Linking the opponents and their case with somebody very unpopular: again this is very popular with politicians. They show that their opponents have unpopular supporters, and sometimes they 'prove' with long quotations that their opponents have the same ideas as someone unpopular. It is irrelevant and dishonest – like attacking a road-building programme because Hitler built roads. Its mirror image is irrelevant authority.

Irrelevant authority

Invoking somebody heroic and popular to support an argument or a course of action: I once heard a local French politician claim that Napoleon supported his scheme for a new town sewer. Unless a living celebrity has directly endorsed an argument, it is dishonest to claim celebrity support for it and even when it is honest it is usually irrelevant. (Who cares what David Beckham thinks about the euro?) A dangerous variant, which is becoming more and more common, is to claim religious authority in support of a secular argument.

I have not said anything yet about quotations. I do not like them, in any speech. Your audience wants to hear your words, not someone else's. Most quotations in speeches are a form of irrelevant authority: your point is no better because Oscar Wilde said it brilliantly. If a quotation is really the most effective way to make your point, by all means use it, but if it is decoration cut it out. If you do use a quotation get it right and attribute it correctly.

Reductio ad absurdum

This is not always a bogus technique. In fact, in its pure form it is a historic rule of formal logic 'not P together with not-P': you should not accept a proposition if its consequences directly contradict itself. Today it is taken more loosely, when speakers try to demolish their opponents by showing that their ideas have 'ridiculous' consequences. There are contexts in which this can be a legitimate form of argument, for example, when a speaker shows that if one person does something it may do no harm but if everybody tried to do it the consequences would be dire.

Reductio ad absurdum can also be used well to make a humorous point. I once heard a speaker teasing her local council which had just announced a proposal to build a tea bar at the town's main bus stop. Why stop at a tea bar, she asked, why not a restaurant, since there was plenty of time to finish a four-course meal while waiting for the bus? Why not build a library so that waiting passengers could catch up on all the great novels they had never finished? Why not build a university, where they could complete a three-year degree course? The 'absurdities' made the point: the council abandoned the plan for a tea bar and spent money improving the bus service.

However, reductio ad absurdum is often used dishonestly to caricature an opponent's position. This often takes the form of a 'slippery slope' argument, often preceded by the words 'the next thing you know'. Here are two examples on both sides of the abortion debate. 'If they let a mother kill her foetus, the next thing you know they'll let her kill her baby because she does not want to keep it, or any other children, or aged parents, or anyone else in her life who is inconvenient . . .' or 'If they take away a woman's right to choose an abortion, the next thing you know they'll take away her right to birth control, and then her right to say no to sex or have any say in how she uses her body.' In this form reductio ad absurdum is very close to the Straw Man.

The straw man

Choosing a particularly weak aspect of the opposing case, or making a complete caricature of it, and then heroically wrestling it to the ground: an example might be 'Fox hunters think they have the right to be cruel to animals. I don't believe that anyone has the right to be cruel to animals and expect the law to leave them alone.' The straw man is often created by False choice (see above) as in 'The opposition think we should do nothing about Saddam Hussein. I think it would be indefensible to let him go on oppressing his people and to let him build up an arsenal of mass destruction.'

If you want to read a particularly fine example of the technique, search on the internet for a speech delivered by Britain's Europe Minister, Peter Hain MP, to the Fabian Society Conference 'A New World Order?' in February

2002. Decide for yourself whether it is legitimate or gives you a sympathy for Mr Hain's opponents.

Tu quoque

You too! Defending your own weaknesses by accusing your opponents of the same: 'I am not taking lectures from the opposition on the misuse of statistics.' A juvenile defence, which will not impress your audience.

With the possible exception of the Common foe and Reductio ad absurdum I think that you should avoid all of these devices. They are debating tricks, and many people will recognize them even if they cannot identify them by name. If you are writing for someone else, you should definitely cut them out, since it is your job to protect your speaker from a reputation for being tricky or slick.

The high moral riposte

If opponents in a live debate use any of these tricks on you, you can often make an effective riposte by actually identifying the trick and shaming your opponents. Something like: 'My opponents have used an old debating trick tonight, the manoeuvre of . . . Most of us learnt that trick at the school debating society. But tonight we're discussing one of the biggest issues for the future of this community and this country and I think we ought to grow out of the school debating society and talk about it like grown-ups . . .'

With luck, no one in the audience will recognize that this too is an old debating trick, namely *Taking the high moral ground*.

SUMMARY

- Think in terms of swaying your audience rather than arguing or persuading.

- Know thoroughly the values and aims of your audience, and what they regard as a source of authority.

- Identify the benefit to your audience of agreeing with you.

- You can analyze your audience thoroughly and use the results without dumbing down or being untrue to yourself.

- Find the common ground between you and your audience, what you both regard as right and reasonable.

- Lead your audience in a logical journey from the common ground to your chosen destination even if you have to begin on their chosen pathway rather than your own.

- With any audience there is always competition either against your choice of common ground or against your choice of journey from it. Understand your competitors, whether visible or invisible.

- Positive arguments for your side are better than negative arguments to destroy your opponents.

- If you have to deal with the opposition case, do so honestly.

- Accept your opponents' good points but show how yours are better.

- Challenge your opponents' bad points with relevant facts whose logic leaves your opponents with no escape. Without such facts, you may have to rely on logic alone.

- Don't use dishonest debating tricks.

- If dishonest tricks are used against you in debate, point them out.

10

The final edit

Removing the barriers against impact

You have by now researched your audience, structured, planned and re-planned your speech, thought of an attention-getting beginning and a rousing finish, composed it, talked it through to yourself, made it rhythmic and colourful, incorporated changes of mood and pace, used well-chosen figures of speech, and if appropriate, routed your opposition thoroughly but fairly, and carried your audience by irresistible logic to their destiny of agreeing with you.

Now write your speech again. Not from scratch but line by line.

Now write your speech again. Not from scratch but line by line. You are going to cut out unnecessary words, clichés and jargon, correct grammar and spelling, check every fact and quotation, clarify obscurities, repair illogicalities and contradictions, and ruthlessly suppress egoism and self-indulgence. At the same time you will check it against your carefully prepared plan. Have you stuck to it and given each element the balance you originally intended? Or, more likely, have you been caught up in the excitement of writing your 'good' passages and thrown the whole speech out of whack?

Have you laid your cuckoo's egg in the nest of another orator?

If you are writing for someone else, you must do these exercises even more thoroughly, especially the ones about ego and self-indulgence. This is a speech for somebody else? Have you sincerely matched his or her strengths and weaknesses or written for yourself by proxy? Have you laid your cuckoo's egg in the nest of another orator?

Cutting out the dead wood

In any body of writing, there are words which contribute absolutely nothing at all to the significance of what is being said.

Take that last sentence. In any 'body of' writing? What does 'body of' contribute? How about 'absolutely nothing at all' (an example of pleonasm) and 'to the significance of what is being said'. That sentence can come down to 'All writing contains unnecessary words' – less than a quarter of the original.

Any writing [at all] can be cut. A fishmonger proudly hangs up a fresh-painted sign: Fresh Fish Sold Here Daily. A kibitzer (critical onlooker) complains at once 'That's ridiculous. You've used far too many words. Look at that Daily. If it's fresh fish you have to sell it daily.' The fishmonger is embarrassed and paints out the Daily. The sign now reads Fresh Fish Sold Here. The kibitzer is still not satisfied. 'Far too many words again. Why say Here? Where else are you selling your fish, in Paris, France?' The fishmonger is embarrassed and paints out the Here. The sign now reads Fresh Fish Sold. The kibitzer frowns. 'Fresh Fish *Sold*? Do people think you give fish away?' The fishmonger is embarrassed and paints out the Sold. The sign now reads Fresh Fish. 'Well, really,' says the kibitzer. 'Do you want them to think you might sell *stale* fish? Of course your fish are fresh.' The fishmonger is embarrassed and paints out the Fresh. The sign now reads Fish. The kibitzer glares. 'Forget the sign, Benny. Anyone can smell your fish a mile away.'

The kibitzer's strategy could make you a very popular speaker. But be ruthless selectively. Keep the essential words of your speech – the Fish.

Talking your speech through and applying the 'conversation test' (see Chapter 5) will give you some help in cutting out unnecessary words but it is not an infallible method. In conversation, we all regularly use unnecessary words (like 'absolutely nothing at all') and we do not automatically edit them into the most direct way of expressing our meaning. When you are looking for dead words, it is worth keeping a special eye out for the following:

1. *The passive*: the passive mood of a verb (the mat was sat on by the cat) is nearly always longer and duller than the active (the cat sat on the

mat). Watch out for the double passive (statistics were ordered to be prepared on the number of cats observed on mats).

2. *Pointless clauses beginning with 'it'*: especially followed by a passive, such as 'it should be remembered that'. If you write and speak well enough, whatever it is will be remembered.

3. *Pleonasms*: 'in this day and age' (today); 'at this moment in time' (now); 'in the final analysis' (ultimately); 'the position in regard to cats' (cats).

4. *Circumlocution*: especially when achieved by piling up abstract nouns (consideration of accessibility issues in relation to transport modes is of paramount importance, in other words, we must think about transport).

5. *Pointless modifiers*: such as *quite* important, *relatively* insignificant. When you use an adjective do not hold back. Another one that comes up quite often, no, often, is the *redundant reinforcer*, trying to add something to a word which is already at maximum strength. Spot the deliberate example in the first paragraph of this chapter.[1]

6. *Entire sentences which repeat something already said*: these can slip through sometimes when there is nothing wrong with them as sentences. 'The report could not attempt to be comprehensive. It deals with some issues more thoroughly than others.' One of those sentences can go.

Grammar

Although you can break some rules of written prose in a speech, you should not break rules of English grammar. Some people think it gives them the common touch to say something like 'me and my friends got on the bus': wrong, it makes them sound ignorant.

> **Every audience contains pedants and there is no reason to annoy them or distract them from your message by bad grammar.**

Every audience contains pedants and there is no reason to annoy them or distract them from your message by bad grammar, and with those pedants in mind you are better off splitting the atom than splitting an infinitive. It is easy to avoid grammatical errors and split infinitives, and even the crew of the

---

[1] It is 'thoroughly' after 'routed'. To 'rout' someone already means to do it thoroughly.

Starship Enterprise should have managed to go boldly rather than to boldly go, which confusingly sounds like a new verb, to boldligo. Pedants also go mad if you make 'media' or 'data' singular: they are plural.

It is not pedantic to be annoyed when a speaker suddenly shifts tenses between past and present or uses a tense confusingly : 'by the year 2000 output is up 20 per cent'. The year 2000 is now history. Change it to 'by the year 2000 output had risen by 20 per cent' or 'in the year 2000 output was 20 per cent higher than . . .' and remember to say higher than what. *Comparisons always need comparators.*

You should spell words properly when you write your speech, even though people will not hear you misspell them. After all, your speech will probably appear in print somewhere, some time. Of course you must not misspell any word in a visual aid.

Clichés

'We must avoid clichés like the plague' was quite a good joke once, and all clichés were once fresh and new. Since you and I never use clichés, the best way to keep alert for them is to listen to other people, especially on the news. Mentally record the phrases that make you cringe because they are so stale and drab – perhaps a politician talking about 'a whole raft of measures', an industrialist talking about 'a strong platform for expansion', anyone at all talking about a 'quantum leap' or 'thinking the unthinkable'? Listen for them in case they infect your own writing.

The nearer it is to death, the harder it is to spot a cliché.

There is a paradox about clichés: the nearer it is to death, the harder it is to spot a cliché. For example, 'leaving no stone unturned' still has a little colour and stands out as a cliché but its companion 'exploring every avenue' has almost no life left and is more likely to survive the editor's pencil. When a cliché is clinically dead, that is when it has lost any link with the concept which first made it fresh and exciting, it may be reborn as a standard term. The expression 'tongue in cheek' has had such a rebirth. It has become a convenient way to describe something said which is provocative but not to be taken seriously.

To help your cliché-hunting, here are a few which I cannot stand:

- . . . needs no introduction from me
- right across the board
- There are no easy answers
- . . . play a [vital] part/have a [vital] part to play
- cold or hard (or both), in relation to facts
- long and hard, in relation to looks
- exploring every option
- pictures or overviews or scenarios of growth and other abstract phenomena
- . . . and their ilk (ilk actually means 'the same', and is not a term of abuse)
- acid or litmus test
- frameworks of any kind except real ones
- better or other half, meaning a partner or spouse
- state of the art
- cutting edge
- step change
- hit the ground running
- almost any sporting allusion outside sport
- all-singing, all-dancing. Once fresh when it described movie musicals, now used regularly in silly contexts ('it will not be an all-singing, all-dancing public inquiry')
- challenges, particularly major challenges, which are not really challenging, as in 'Car parking is a major challenge for the airport'.

Jargon

It is sometimes right to use jargon. Every occupation, every branch of human life, has its special vocabulary which may be the only correct or instant way to convey a particular idea. If a lawyer uses the word 'consideration' instead of 'price', if a doctor says 'haematoma' instead of 'bruise', if a bridge player says 'ruff', if a cricketer talks about an 'outswinger' and a baseball player about a 'curve ball' these people all have a good reason. People who really need correct and instant communication use jargon all the time – listen to any aircraft pilot.

It is sometimes right to use jargon. Bain McKay, a practitioner of the new science of Knowledge Management, has defended specialists' jargon in these stirring terms:

> **Jargon is a key cornerstone of Knowledge Management. More importantly, it's a key underpinning to learning and leveraging knowledge. Interestingly enough, a taxonomy is a jargon vocabulary of shortcuts that experts use to iconify conceptually classified meaningful patterns, so they can cover ground very quickly – that is, more productively. It's part of the abstraction process we all go through as we learn a discipline and abstract it into anchors and hooks to tie associated concepts together into internally visualized patterns of 7+/–2 scoped hierarchies.**

By all means use jargon when there is no other way to explain what you mean. But be certain that your audience can understand it. Take special care with jargon words which have an everyday meaning. If you are a computer specialist, you know that a 'field' is an area in a fixed or known location in a unit of data such as a record, message header or computer instruction, which has a purpose and usually a fixed size but your audience may think first of an area with cows. Take even greater care with acronyms, which can have dozens of different meanings. Unless your audience consists entirely of pilots, do not use GP for 'glide path' – say the words in full and no one will think 'general practitioner' in Britain or 'general purpose' in the United States. Acronyms are especially hard work for foreign audiences unless they have been internationally agreed.

However, you must be ruthless with unnecessary jargon, particularly the buzz words which have evolved to give trivial thoughts the air of science. The following words or phrases are known to have inspired loathing and mass hysteria:

- architecture (in politics, economics, management science)
- B2B, B2C (business-to-business, business-to-consumer)
- benchmark
- best practice, best value
- core competences, missions or tasks
- deliver for anything other than groceries, packages and speeches, and even worse, deliverables
- drivers not in vehicles as in 'technology is a key driver of economic growth' and all adjectives formed with -driven (customer-driven)
- empowerment and enablement
- fast-track
- first-mover
- focus and all adjectives formed with -focused (mission-focused)
- -grounded (as in theory-grounded)
- input, especially as verb
- -ize (new verbs formed with -ize, especially optimize, maximize, incentivize, utilize, prioritize, diarize, diurnalize: try not to use any verb in -ize which is less than 50 years old)
- key (when used as adjective in isolation to mean 'crucial', as in 'derivatives are key to the group's success')
- knowledge-based
- leading edge
- leverage, as verb
- next-generation
- -oriented or worse, -orientated (as in team-oriented)
- out of the loop or outside the box or envelope
- ownership, not in precise everyday sense but as piece of psycho-socio babble meaning 'has some sense of involvement in'. Recently I heard a police officer say 'The community has now taken ownership of the murder.'

- paradigm, especially a new one or a paradigm shift. However, it is permissible to sing this word, in the modern classic 'Buddy, can you paradigm?'

- pilot as verb not attached to aircraft, as in 'We have been chosen to pilot the Best Value initiative.' However, if the initiative is -grounded in any way (see above) it may never take off.

- proactive

- seamless

- segue

- stakeholder – actually quite a useful shorthand for people who have some interest in some phenomenon, but unbearably smug and smarmy. Whenever I hear the word 'stakeholder' I reach for my revolver.

- synergy

- 24/7/365

- win-win

Have you noticed how much jargon overlaps with cliché?

The most dangerous word of all

One word is even more dangerous to a speech than the worst jargon or gobbledygook. It is neither long nor obscure. It is the word 'I'. Check your pronouns as you edit your speech. If it is seething with I's and me's, there is something wrong. You are talking about yourself not speaking to the audience. You's are almost as dangerous. If your speech is full of you's, it makes you sound like a platoon sergeant barking orders at the audience.

Take special care these days with the pronouns 'he' and 'she'. It really is bad manners and a tactical error to use only 'he' if you also mean 'she'. (However you may retain 'he' alone if the reference is uncomplimentary, so that criminals, incompetents or generally obnoxious and over-mighty people can be reserved for men.) A profusion of he, she, it or they may mean that you are too distant from your audience. It is a sign that your speech is about an *outside* world to you and your audience, not sharing a common world.

Your speech should have a good supply of we's. If you cannot find many we's when you edit your speech, try to slip some in. But do not pretend to be part of a we-community with your audience if you are not. Do not say 'we sailors' if you are a landlubber. Look for a community which you share with the audience even if it is living in the same country or the same century.

All your little darlings must be killed

This was a famous maxim by a great writer, William Faulkner, and it is the saddest part of editing.

The first things you should look to cut are those which most delight you. The hilarious story, the sparkling one-liner, the fascinating speculation, the dazzling metaphor – be ruthless with them all.

There is a bleak logic to Faulkner's advice. If something appeals to you *as writing* then its form has almost certainly become more powerful than its content. Moreover if something appeals very deeply to you, it probably means something special to you which your audience will not share. Put those two thoughts together, and it is likely that your little darlings are a barrier not a bridge between you and your audience. Moreover, they are probably making your speech too long and interrupting its logic. Little darlings, like spoilt children, demand attention and special favours. They will not slip unobtrusively into your speech but force you to make room for them, not only through extra words but in additional logic to provide a reason for them being there.

I put one deliberate example of a 'little darling' into this book (although you may detect many others). In the last chapter, in the section on 'Ad hominem' arguments, I told a story about Governor Huey Long. I have always loved that story and I was determined to work it in. But he adds nothing to my point, he demands extra words and I had to put in an extra, irrelevant reason for having him there (audiences do not care about lying politicians).

That is the kind of little darling which must be killed. If you are certain that your favourite passages will have a matching impact on your audience by all means leave them in. If you are uncertain, try them out in rehearsal and let your rehearsal audience decide their fate.

Fortunately, little darlings are survivors. If you have to kill one in one speech, store it for another.

If you are writing for someone else, you have a moral duty to cut out your cherished passages, as well as a literary one. You have no right to leave your little darlings on someone else's doorstep.

SUMMARY

- You must edit your first draft with minute care, line by line.
- Cut out dead words and sentences which contribute no extra meaning. You will need to use your eye as well as your ear.
- Use correct grammar.
- Be vigilant against clichés, especially those very nearly dead.
- Use jargon if it is essential to your meaning, destroy it when it is not.
- Check pronouns for excessive I's and you's and sexist he's. Make sure that your speech has some legitimate we's.
- Murder your little darlings, especially if you are writing for someone else.

11

Rehearse, and again I say, rehearse

Effective rehearsal, alone and with others

Your speech is now written, rewritten and edited. You must now rehearse it as often as possible, alone and in company. There is no excuse for not rehearsing, however busy you are, however familiar the speech you intend to deliver.

Rehearsal is an endless process of discovery. By rehearsing you will discover any late errors in your writing and your facts, and you will discover more words which you can cut. You will discover whether your jokes work and why they don't, and in general whether your speech will work on your listeners' hearts and minds as you intend it to. You will discover the right pitch of your voice and eliminate irritating vocal mannerisms (you know . . . like . . . that is . . . er . . .) and physical gestures. You will master any visual aids you are using, and whether or not you are able to rehearse in the actual setting you might be able to rehearse with any sound system which it uses.

> **Rehearsal is an endless process of discovery.**

Above all, by rehearsing you will get control of your nerves.

Before rehearsing you have one important decision to make. Will you speak from your full text or from notes?

Notes or text?

Every speaker needs at least one speaking note. Make an essential card. Write on a special, unforgettable card the name and title of your host, the name of the organizations you are speaking to, the name of anyone else you have to thank and the place where you are. Put this card in your speaking materials.

If you have a great memory, an accomplished delivery, complete self-confidence and iron self-discipline you *can* deliver a speech without any further note. But there are too many risks that one of these things will let you down. You will forget something you intended to say, especially the killer fact that demolishes the opposing position and the inescapable logic that supports your own, you will develop irritating mannerisms, you will stumble and ramble, you will dry up and panic. Even if none of these happen, there are two other major risks of speaking without a note. First, your audience, even if only subconsciously, may find it ill-mannered. No notes could signify no care: 'He came to us and he just gave the same speech he must have said a thousand times before.' (The 'he' in that last sentence is deliberate: I have never seen a female speaker give that impression to an audience.) Second, even if your audience do not think it rude, they may be so awestruck by your performance that they do not remember anything you say.

For all of these reasons, I think that all speakers should take some speaking materials with them. The choice is the full text or notes.

Full text

The full text is essential if you are speaking on the record. If you are stating your government's position to the Security Council of the United Nations, you simply cannot afford to make a mistake. The same is true if you are being reported in any media. If your time is very tight and it is terribly important to cover every point, it is also prudent to use the full text. Finally, if you are inexperienced as a speaker or very nervous, you may need the full text like the stabilizers on your first bicycle.

The full text is essential if you are speaking on the record.

Using a full text is a mark of respect to any audience, for it is a sign that you have taken trouble over them. However, it is heavy-handed for a social speech at an intimate occasion, and the sight of a thick mound of paper in your hand will cause sinking hearts in any audience. If you use notes, they will not know how long your speech is going to last, and there is always some hope that it will end soon. But if they can see the mound shrinking only slowly they will know that they are trapped with you for some time.

The full text carries some other serious penalties. The obvious one is that you will have to read it. You will have to look at the text and lose eye contact with your audience. You will also have to change pages. Meet this problem in advance by telling your host that you will be speaking from a full text. The host might even be able to offer you the chance to use an autocue – the karaoke machine of public speaking. Your speech will be in front of you, word for word, but with no barrier between you and the audience. You can be totally in command and, at the same time, totally spontaneous. Failing an autocue, you will need some kind of platform for a full text, wide enough to let you switch pages easily and as high as it will go without obscuring your face. You will want to look up from your text as often and as quickly as you can to gain contact with the audience. The old-fashioned lectern was designed with these things in mind.

If you are using a full text make it as easy to read as possible. Put it on good thick white paper. Have it typed in your favourite typeface (most typefaces with serifs are easier to read than those without. Serifs are the little extra 'hooks' on letters: this is a serif face, this one is not. Sans-serifs look modern and dynamic and they are better for short phrases in a visual aid but serifs are easier to read in a text.

Use at least a 12-point font, and at least double-spacing. Leave a big margin on either side, for last-minute notes. Write your speech out in exactly the same style you would use for print: in other words, don't write it out ONLY IN CAPITAL LETTERS, use normal punctuation, and don't abbreviate. Number each page clearly.

Find a consistent scheme for indicating degrees of emphasis, probably <u>underlining</u> for important words or phrases and **bold for super-duper important words or phrases**. If you are using long quotations, make them look different from the rest of the text, by indenting or spacing. Find a consistent scheme for telling you when and how you intend to use a visual aid.

End each line with a complete word, end each page with a complete sentence. Do not spread a quotation over more than one page.

It is dangerous to write stage directions on your text. You may read them out (an American politician once began a speech with the words 'Message: I Care'). If you must use stage directions, minimize this risk by writing them out in manuscript. Also use manuscript to indicate any passages you might cut out in an emergency. Whether or not you have any stage directions, **keep your actual speaking text separate from any copies you might be handing out.**

It is dangerous to write stage directions on your text.

Do not use the last third of any page – then you will not have to look down so much.

Do not staple or bind your pages. Instead use a reliable paperclip. If you cannot see a paperclip without turning it into sculpture, carry lots of spares.

Keep your speech clean (in every sense). Put it a crumpleproof folder which can resist grime, rain, food and drink.

Even if you are using the full text, do not forget the essential card with the people to thank and the place where you are.

Notes

Notes will give you far more spontaneity, and more chance of bonding with your audience. Everyone has his or her own style of note-taking, and it is not my place to say use this format or another. But some general advice might be helpful.

First, and most important, since you have taken great trouble to write your speech, your notes should *bring back to you what you intend to deliver.* They may not bring back your speech word for word (although you may want to write out vital passages in full, even if you are using notes). But your notes must be enough to bring you instant recall of the basic architecture of your speech, which we discussed in Chapter 4. They must tell you exactly what you are going to cover in each section: Introduction, Beginning, Middle, Ending. They must bring back any jokes or anecdotes you intend to risk, and indeed any kind of illustration of your themes. If you aim to sway your audience, your notes must make your own logic totally clear to you (otherwise how can it possibly be clear to your audience?) and let you use any killer facts fluently, logically and accurately. Finally and of course, your notes must make it clear how and when you are going to use any visual aids.

Second, no matter what notes you use, it is terribly helpful and reassuring to have *your complete speech in outline on one sheet of paper.* The ideal thing is to get onto one sheet the final version of the speech plan which you made after reading Chapter 4. It may be hard to squeeze the full plan onto one sheet even though print uses less space than manuscript. If so, remember what you want to remember: the structure of your speech is more important than the fine detail. Therefore try not to lose the hierarchy of headings and sub-headings you prepared for your plan. Make sure you can read the outline comfortably and leave plenty of white space around it. Put it on good quality white paper and keep it clean and safe.

You may find you can manage with just your outline speech in front of you – together with the essential card. If not, you will have to supplement it with note cards. You might use a note card to write down verbatim a key passage, or a precise version of any killer fact or simply to pick out points in detail which you cannot include on the outline speech. You might also want to use a separate card for each visual aid. The annoying thing about note cards is that they never have a right size. Big ones do not fit into your pocket, little ones give you no space to write in and get lost all the time. Pick a size which allows you to use big handwriting and still keep plenty of white space. Above all, pick a stiff, durable card.

If you use cards, make sure that you know exactly where the information on each card belongs in the speech, Introduction, Beginning, Middle, End, and don't force yourself to return to any card after you have used it once. Mark each card with a number and cross-refer to it in your outline.

Put in one blank card – Card Zero – and use it to jot down any points which demand an instant reply before your formal introduction. Do *not* use the essential card for this purpose. When you have finished the cards, do *not* bind them together in any way, but keep them together with a firm rubber band. If you cannot handle a rubber band without making it a weapon or a musical instrument, keep a lot of spares.

If you have to use more than ten cards as well as your outline you are probably better off working from the full text.

The major problem about using notes is simply that you may not be able to read them fluently, and you may lose your way in your speech. There are some other risks: notes are easy to lose and because they are always unfinished, you may be tempted to amend them at the last minute, and your crossings-out and scrawlings-in may make them illegible. Even if you do use notes, carry a full version of your speech for emergency use, apart from any copies you may be taking to hand out.

It is a personal choice whether you want the security and precision of speaking from the full text or the spontaneity and extra audience contact you get from speaking from notes. This is one of the issues you can resolve by rehearsal.

Rehearsal – be honest

There are many ways to achieve the objectives of rehearsal, both alone and in front of others, but in all cases you must be completely honest with yourself. A rehearsal shows up flaws, either in yourself or in your speech, and they may be equally hard to admit.

After the time you have spent in preparing it, your speech by now will be a work of art to you – so brilliantly constructed, so fascinating in its exposition, so logical in its arguments, so powerful in its emotions, so dazzling in its wordplay – and it will be unbearable to admit that it is not. And as for you – the charismatic, silver-tongued, spell-binding author – is that really you with the sad hair, and grinding voice, and the weak gestures and the irritating mannerisms? If you cannot bear to make such discoveries, do not rehearse, but in that case do not speak either.

Rehearsal can be especially painful if you are writing for somebody else. Your words will be more precious to you when someone else is speaking them, and it is even harder to admit that there is something wrong with them. Just as a playwright is tempted to blame the actors for lines which do not work, you will be tempted to blame the speaker. But you do not have the same status as a playwright; as a speech-writer you are an anonymous worker and it is your job to provide words which work *for your speaker*. If he or she makes a mistake or a fumble with your material, *it is your fault*. Be prepared to fix it – or cut it.

However, some weaknesses may be the speaker's fault, not yours. He or she may have a weak, dull voice, or gabble, or use annoying gestures, or wear the wrong clothes, or simply come over as uninteresting and unappealing. You may find it very hard to tell him or her these things. You may genuinely like him or her (and in case I have not told you earlier, do *not* write for someone you actually dislike. It is unfair on both of you). You may be afraid of an outburst of temper, but speech-writing is no career for wimps. You may even be afraid of losing your commission or your job, but speech-writing is no career for sycophants either.

If your speaker is doing something wrong, it is your job to say so. You can find tactful ways of doing this. For example, for a weak delivery you might say: 'When you first tried that passage, you gave it a lot more emphasis. It sounded more like' [now read it properly] 'I wondered if you had decided to tone it down, because it did work so well the first

If your speaker is doing something wrong, it is your job to say so.

time.' A good ploy for correcting an irritating gesture is to use or invent ethnic expertise: 'I notice you use that hand chopping gesture a lot. I'm worried that there might be some [name significant ethnic group] in the audience because in their culture that gesture is terribly offensive.' For terrible clothing you might suggest that your speaker's choice would clash with the décor of the setting (or show up badly on television, if the cameras are going to be there) or simply that he/she looks so much better in blue.

However you soften the blow, do not hide the truth. Rehearsal is a time for total honesty, from the speaker and all the hired help.

Rehearsal techniques

Part of being honest in rehearsal is about simulating your speaking conditions as far as possible. That means that in any setting you must rehearse your speech *out loud*, standing up, and *at the pace you intend to deliver it*. (Actors sometimes gabble lines to memorize them, but you are a speaker not an actor and you should not be trying to memorize your speech.) Moreover, if you have decided already to speak from the full text or from notes, use the method on which you have settled. Try to wear the clothes you are going to wear, or something like them. Match the physical environment of your speech as much as you can.

Another vital point for rehearsals: *don't stop and never look back*. If you stumble keep on until you reach the end of your speech, or at least the end of the particular segment you intended to rehearse. Speaking out loud and at the right pace is the only way to be accurate about the time you take, while speaking on in rehearsal makes you far less likely to dry up in the real thing.

Remember that rehearsal is for *speaking* not for rewriting. If you think on your feet of something brilliantly new, do not stop to write it down but push on with your speech. It is probably a 'little darling' anyway, and if it is not you will not forget it. Do not stop for the opposite reason, to cut something you suddenly recognize as weak or unnecessary. Speak on. As you become more practised in speaking, you will be able to make these instant off-the-cuff adjustments. But if you cannot yet manage them, do not let them break the flow of your speech, either in rehearsal or the real thing.

If you rehearse *alone* do it in front of a mirror and switch on a tape recorder. It is a good idea to switch on the radio softly at the same time, to simulate background noise. Do not even look at your text to

Be honest – are you presentable, never mind commanding?

begin with. Gaze into the mirror as if waiting for the applause to die down and your audience to be still. Now see what the audience would see. Be honest – are you presentable, never mind commanding? Are you making good eye contact with yourself and holding it for at least 20 seconds?

Now start speaking but glimpse at yourself in the mirror as often as you can. What are you like? Gestures, movements, mannerisms – what do they say about you? Be honest.

Keep the tape recorder running and get to the end of your speech, however much you stumble. Look at your watch. If you are running over time junk some material altogether, even if you promised it to your imaginary audience in the introduction, but do *not* speed up. When you have reached the end, hold your gaze in front of the mirror, and receive the applause. Then sit down and play the tape if you have the nerve.

Play the tape right through without stopping. Note the time. Add a couple of minutes more for the actual speech. Are you too long (likely) or too short (very unlikely)?

Compare the tape to your final text. Mark up any passages in the text where you stumbled or which you even omitted altogether. Keep alert for any vital words you omitted – such as 'not'. Underline them in your written text. Keep alert for pointless fillers you may have added in. Mark up passages which sound dull on the tape and those which sound exciting.

Finally, listen to your voice as well as your words. Get over the shock of hearing it as others do, not as you hear it yourself. Judge the voice on the tape – clear, pleasant, varied, animated? Are there any annoying mannerisms or vocal tics? Are there any words persistently mispronounced?

If you rehearse *with other people* you can do these jobs a hundred times better. For a start, you might get someone to put you on video, which will record not only your impossible vocalisms but your dreadful gestures. Other people are much better than you alone at deciding whether you are audible or vocally interesting. Other people will have fresh eyes and ears for mistakes in grammar and style which have survived your editing.

Moreover, *only other people* can decide whether your speech makes sense. You know too much about your subject and you will have lived with your speech for too long. Only rehearsal with other people will identify passages which are obscure or illogical or simply boring.

If you rehearse with a small group of people, make sure that at least two of them have never heard the speech before or worked on it in any way. Give everyone in the group a copy of the text as you intend to deliver it. You might like to invite different people to monitor different things, voice, gestures and mannerisms. If there are to be interventions, or questions and answers, get everyone to put you a likely intervention or question. Always ask someone new to listen to the speech for sense and interest and ask someone else to mark up on the text copy every place where you stumbled or added, omitted or amended something. (The main speech-writer should do this job if you were not the author.)

After every rehearsal, of course, you need honest feedback about your strengths and weaknesses. You will try to eliminate your weaknesses for the next rehearsal (coming chapters may give you some ideas). But treat every rehearsal as new, rather than as trying to correct the specific faults of the previous one.

At least one rehearsal must be a technical rehearsal, including the use of any visual aids. If you cannot rehearse in the actual setting, at least find out what equipment it uses and practise speaking with that or something like it.

Everybody has only a fixed quota of stage fright. Do not be alarmed if you seem to get worse and worse at rehearsal. All rehearsals will make the actual speech better and there is some truth in the cliché that a bad dress rehearsal makes for a good show. I have a theory that everybody has only a fixed quota of stage fright and the more that quota is used up in rehearsal the less there is available for the actual performance.

My partner bore out that theory last year when she had to give an important technical speech to an expert committee of the British House of Lords. She rehearsed constantly, with myself and friends, for days and days and with worse and worse results. The dress rehearsal ended in tears. The actual speech was a knockout.

SUMMARY

- You cannot rehearse a speech too much.
- Decide before rehearsing whether you want to speak from a full text or from notes. A full text is essential if every word of your speech is essential and is going on the record. It will give you more confidence if you are nervous.
- Notes will give you more spontaneity and more opportunity to develop rapport with the audience. If notes do not work for you in rehearsal you may go back to a full text.
- Always make and carry an essential card to remind you where you are and whom to thank.
- Make a full text easy to read, using the conventions of written language. Keep your speaking version to yourself. If you use a full text make certain that the venue has somewhere you can read it conveniently and without losing too much contact with the audience. ▶

- Your notes should be enough to give you recall of the structure and logic of your speech and all the key material you intend to put in it, including the timing of any visual aids. It is very valuable to have a complete outline of your speech in front of you on one sheet of paper. The plan you prepared before writing your speech is ideal.
- If you supplement this outline with detailed notes on cards, make certain you know exactly where you will be using each card. Do not use any card more than once in your speech.
- Be totally honest in rehearsals, with yourself and with your speaker.
- Rehearse your speech standing up, aloud, at the right pace, in conditions as near as possible to the actual setting. Don't stop if you make or see a mistake – complete the speech or at least one passage.
- If you are rehearsing alone, you can use a mirror and tape recorder to check your appearance, gestures, mannerisms, vocal tics – and, above all, your timing.
- Other people can give you much better feedback on your performance than you can alone. Only other people can say whether all parts of your speech are interesting and make sense.
- Even awful rehearsals are valuable, not least for coming to grips with stage fright.

12

Delivery

Fighting nerves, standing tall, speaking well,
coping with disasters

This chapter has a few suggestions for overcoming stage fright, for moving and standing well and for using your voice well. Each of these issues is a special subject in its own right: people write books about them and give expert advice, tuition and treatment. I am an amateur in all of them. I can only claim that these suggestions have worked for me and for people I know. I hope that they work for you, so that you can do justice to the brilliant words which you can now create.

The man with egg on his suit

Through your superb writing and your meticulous and honest rehearsals you have given yourself the best possible inoculation against stage fright. But even so you may still be overcome and need some kind of remedy before you begin to speak.

If you do get stage fright, remember first that you are in good company. According to a recent poll, Americans are more frightened of public speaking than anything else, including death. Napoleon suffered from stage fright before speaking, so did Winston Churchill.

Some years ago I watched Michael Heseltine in action, one of the most successful orators in modern British politics. He had a friendly, even adoring, audience to speak to, but his hands shook and his knuckles turned white when he gripped the lectern.

There is a theory that stage fright is linked to genius and that must be true – after all, look how badly *you* get it. In the whole of American history, only one president has ever claimed to enjoy public speaking. He was Warren G. Harding (1920–23), who gave it the engaging name of 'bloviating'. Harding generally figures in the bottom ten of American presidents. All the undisputed great presidents found public speaking an ordeal. So if you are nervous before speaking, congratulate yourself on being Lincoln not Harding.

Apart from thinking about the famous company you share, the first rule for dealing with stage fright is to recognize it. The symptoms of stage fright can be dramatic and reinforce each other. The thought of

The symptoms of stage fright can be dramatic and reinforce each other.

speaking to the audience makes you nervous. Your hands start shaking. You are now doubly nervous: not only will the audience hear you make a bad speech but they will see your hands shaking. Your throat now tightens and your stomach starts churning – more things which the audience will notice, more things to worry about. (One symptom of stage fright, incidentally, is the belief that the audience knows everything about you, including things for which there is no outward evidence, like a churning stomach.)

It may help you to know that all of these things are meant to happen. They are the product of natural, chemical reactions which enabled the human species to survive when threatened by mammoths or sabre-toothed tigers. The mammoths and tigers never got stage fright, and look where they are.

If that does not ease off the symptoms, there are a number of well-tested techniques you can try to control them. If your muscles are tensing up, try sitting in a chair and deliberately tensing each muscle in sequences from head to toe. Think of nothing but the tension in that muscle, crank it up as high as it will go, count slowly to three and let the tension go, make the muscle floppy. If you are lucky enough to have a partner with you, get him or her to give you a massage.

Relax your facial muscles by yawning and making funny faces. If your arms, knees and legs are shaking, make them shake deliberately and then go floppy. If your hands are hot, rinse them in cold water, if they are cold, rub them together. In general terms, obey your body's instructions: if you are thirsty, have a glass of water (nothing stronger); if you are hungry or feeling sick to your stomach, have a little chocolate or fruit. Take any opportunity to go to the lavatory.

Some people like to escape from the nerve-wracking speaking environment by visualizing an ideal setting, either imaginary or one they know. Other people prefer to concentrate intensely on one tiny part of the setting – patterns in fabric, an old photograph, a name on a notice. One of the best ways of escaping your own feelings is to be interested in other people's. Start with your host. What does the event mean to him or her? What represents a success or a disaster? Talk to other people – why are they here, have they come before, what do they hope or fear from the event? At worst you will be distracted, at best you will discover that the audience are really quite nice people, and they want you to succeed.

Many people overcome stage fright by listening to music, either real or in their heads, or by meditating or, if they are religious, by prayer.

It is an excellent idea to read something aloud before you begin your speech. But do not use any of your own words. Take with you your favourite piece of poetry or prose and then read it like a ham actor – exaggerate all your mouth and facial movements, give full value to all the vowels, bite off each consonant. This will convince you that you have not dried up completely, it will also exercise your vocal chords, and prepare you to speak expressively.

If you do have stage fright, it is important to change the balance in your mind between yourself and the audience. They are not the enemy, they are not all-powerful and all-knowing and they have no dominion over you. Remind yourself constantly what a great person you are, how lucky they are to have you, what a superb speech you are about to give them.

Check your appearance minutely at the last possible moment before speaking.

Begin this mental preparation early, by dressing and grooming yourself faultlessly. In the light of the conventions of your audience, dress in a way that conveys respect but do so at your highest range of affordable elegance. Take special care with personal hygiene and grooming, and all your accessories. Check your appearance minutely at the last possible moment before speaking.

Apart from making you feel better, dressing carefully is an excellent distraction. My old university, Oxford, is aware of this. For examinations, it makes its undergraduates wear an absurd costume called subfusc, which they will never have to wear again in their entire lives. Assembling subfusc is a bore and an anxiety on examination day – but it takes one's mind off the exams. Trick yourself in the same way, by picking over your clothes. If you can, give yourself a last-minute choice to make by packing alternative ties, scarves, accessories or jewellery.

Even if you are not planning to use it to deliver your speech, take a full text with you and look at it. You have had it faultlessly printed and bound, so admire it as a precious artefact. Is it not marvellous of you to share it with them?

You might also enjoy composing a press release for yourself. Go back to Chapter 8, reread the definition of hyperbole, and create the most hysterically flattering account of your speech. If you need a model, read an official account of the receptions given to speeches by the late North Korean leader, Kim Il-Sung. 'A packed audience at the Sylvain Legwinski Auditorium sat spellbound/cheered unceasingly/choked with laughter/wept tears of joy when [you] spoke on . . .' However, if you actually write out this press release, do not make the mistake of releasing it to the press.

Finally, if the audience is still getting on top of you, try a technique which never fails. Look for the man with egg on his suit (and/or the woman with the impossible make-up). There is always at least one in every crowd. You cannot feel frightened by a man with egg on his suit (that is why, subliminally, people throw eggs at politicians) or overawed by a woman with impossible make-up.

Somewhere in there you should find a remedy for stage fright which works for you. But remember also that some things never work, for anybody. The first is alcohol: you may imagine you speak better after a few drinks, but you do not. At best alcohol slows you down, at worst it makes you lose the plot. In fact no drug at all, lawful or unlawful, makes you speak better, including caffeine and so-called energy drinks. Apart from its terrible effect on your voice and breathing, nicotine will also throw you into conflict with the anti-smokers in the host organization or your audience. Any heavy meal is bad for speaking and cheese is especially bad for the vocal chords. So are very cold drinks.

Voice

One of the components of stage fright is a terror that one's voice is inadequate. Of course it is not. Your voice has carried you through millions of successful conversations, and it will carry you through your speeches in the same way.

If you have written well, and talked out your speech as you wrote it, you should have gone a long way to using the strengths of your voice. If your speech has any rhythm and pace and colour it will virtually force your voice to respond. You should also have edited out, with the help of rehearsal, any words which you persistently mispronounce, and any dead fillers and irritating vocal mannerisms. Rehearsals should also have corrected any tendency to gabble or to drag.

Even after rehearsals, you may still want to work on the pitch, pace and variety of your voice. Begin by learning to control your breathing, and begin that by having somebody check your posture both sitting and standing. He or she should be looking for tension and unnatural twists in any part of your body. Your head should be still and look comfortable, and maintaining eye contact with the audience without twisting your neck.

Even after rehearsals, you may still want to work on the pitch, pace and variety of your voice.

When you are holding a comfortable balanced posture, either standing or sitting, practise breathing in different rhythms, using different intervals to breathe in and out. Give yourself the power to breathe slowly. Feel your diaphragm (just below your ribs) and make sure that you are breathing from deep down in your abdomen not short, sharp breaths in your chest. Take the previous page of this book and read it out loud. When you come to take a breath, say out loud 'Breathe'. Control the intervals, so that this coincides with natural breaks in the page.

An exercise which combines breathing and pitch is to sing parts of your speech like a psalm. Go to the piano, and start off singing sentences to different notes. When you have arrived at a starting note which lets you sing comfortably, that is a good natural pitch for your voice.

If you think your voice lacks expression, do repeat the exercise we looked at a moment ago. Be a ham actor. Exaggerate everything you can, in both sounds and sense. Do this first with your favourite piece of poetry or prose then work down to more ordinary writing, perhaps a page from this book. Make it sound like Victorian melodrama. Pretend that it is tragic, or funny, or inspiring. Now do the traditional trick of declaim-

Be a ham actor. ing the telephone directory. Tape the results. They will be hilarious, but amazing. You will discover powers of articulation and expression you had never believed. You can and should transfer those powers to your speech-making.

For although we discussed earlier how a speech is conversation, speaking in public demands a little more effort than an intimate conversation. You have a larger space to fill and human beings deaden your sound and compete with sounds of their own, you hope no more than coughs or shuffling feet. You will therefore have to do everything a little better than you do in ordinary speech, better diction, better penetration, better expression. So give a ham actor's version of yourself.

For a simple experiment in pacing, read the following passage out loud at different speeds:

" George Orwell would be despondent but not surprised by the state of the English language today. In *1984*, he predicted the phenomenon of 'duckspeak', words intended to mean nothing and designed to show mindless acceptance of the values and mentality of its originators. Orwell's 'duckspeak' was originated by the ruling party in a totalitarian dictatorship. It was part of the general phenomenon of Newspeak, language so shrivelled in meaning that it would not allow people to think differently from the ruling party.

Although we do not have a one-party state, we hear even more duckspeak than Orwell predicted. It is created not only by governments but by various professions and special interest groups, and for the same reason as Orwell's in *1984*. Duckspeak serves to identify people who are totally loyal to the values of the originating group, and it deprives them of the chance to think any other way. "

This passage is exactly 150 words long. At a normal rate of speech and without mistakes you should get through it in exactly one minute. Measure the times at different speeds and note when the passage became ponderous and boring (too slow) or unintelligible (too fast). Make a note of when the passage sounded just right – probably a little over a minute because it is quite complex, and to deliver it clearly you would normally slow your delivery.

Judicious silence has a mesmeric effect on an audience.

Finally remember that the most powerful thing you can do with your voice is not to use it at all. Judicious silence has a mesmeric effect on an audience. Build pauses into your speech. Always have them before you begin, and then have some more at moments when you want an idea to sink in. Experiment in company with different lengths of pause. When does your audience start to feel uncomfortable?

Damn microphones

All microphones without exception are irritating. Avoid them if you possibly can, and refuse point-blank to use a hand-held microphone (you need your hands for better things). If your audience is 40 or less, you should be able to manage without a microphone.

A clip-on microphone is less obtrusive and allows you to move. But it is still something of a tether: you have to remember where the cord is and to avoid disconnecting it. If you are stuck with a fixed microphone you simply have to stay at the right distance from it and keep your head turned to it.

Insist on testing any microphone before you speak.

Insist on testing any microphone before you speak. Read long passages into it at different volumes and speeds. Have an accomplice at the back of the hall and make certain he or she can hear you well. Get the microphone exactly right for you: if it is a fixed one, put it at the height which allows your best standing position and lets you adjust your gaze freely between your text or notes and the audience.

With any microphone your voice will lose some clarity. You will have to speak more slowly and with exaggerated diction. You also will have to control your volume – too loud and you will treat your audience to a feedback screech.

If you are asked a question, always repeat it into the microphone. It is always a good idea to repeat the question; it is good manners to the questioner and it gives you time to think.

Microphones are treacherous. They amplify not only your chosen words but your unchosen ones – muttered asides, curses, private jokes (including cynical cutting comments on your host and audience). If you have not learnt to cut these out, you deserve to have them amplified over the microphone. For the same reason, you should also eliminate paper shuffling, finger drumming, sniffs, coughs and belches.

'Every little movement tells a story of its own'

This was the chorus of an old-time variety song and it is true. What your audience sees is at least as important to them as what they hear. If a speaker delivers a fine sermon about trust and integrity but twists constantly and cannot maintain eye contact with the audience, which message will be believed?

Learn to make a good opening impression. My former employer Denis Healey has never cured himself of one annoying mannerism. Whenever he feels that he has delivered a particularly brilliant line he turns aside and smirks horribly at an imaginary enraptured listener offstage. If you must have such an imaginary friend please seat him or her in the audience.

At rehearsals you should have discovered what kind of movements and gestures work for you, but the following principles may also give you some help.

First, learn to make a good opening impression. Rehearse walking on to the platform. If you are already on the platform, rehearse standing up at the right moment and walking to the podium. All of these movements should be measured and calm and you should maintain eye contact with the audience as you make them. Enjoy the hysterical applause, but do not milk it or choke it off.

Get yourself completely ready to speak, in your own time, arranging your text or notes and standing in a comfortable position with your head held high but not craning upwards. Gaze over your audience without speaking, focusing at the back of the room. In the silence between the end of the hysterical applause and the awkward shuffling of feet, begin your speech.

In the body of your speech there is no *need* for gestures. If you stand still and keep regular eye contact with the audience you will communicate far better than twist-

Stillness conveys authority.

ing and waving your hands. Stillness conveys authority. The most powerful gesture of all is pausing and standing still. Make and hold eye contact in each pause with a different member of the audience.

If you must make gestures the golden rule is to make them big and decisive, and long enough for people to see them and take them in. Yet again, be a ham actor. Make your body express Attitudes with a capital letter: Anger, Incredulity, Playfulness. If you make a hand gesture, start it from the shoulder not the elbow, and never point across your body or your face.

Certain gestures are clichés – which is their great strength. People know exactly what they mean. Pointing finger: look over there. Sustained pointing finger: accusation. Hand out, palm up: new idea coming, worth listening to. Hand out, palm down, contemptuous sweep: idea was rubbish, forget it. Counting on fingers: list of points (another reason why three is such a good number for lists, you can use your three biggest fingers). Hand out in stop sign: stop or calm down.

Gestures are dangerous with a multinational audience, because they mean different things to different cultures. A perfect excuse for standing still.

Coping with emergencies

All kinds of things can go wrong with your speech. Some will be obvious to your audience (power failure, noise, audience member taken ill, child or animal on

Do not panic. These things happen.

the loose); others will not (previous speaker overruns/uses all your material, major event makes your speech obsolete, you make a mistake).

Do not panic. These things happen. You cannot call yourself a public speaker until you have had to compete with a runaway mouse.

If the audience is sharing the emergency, wait for it to be dealt with. If there are any victims make sure that they have received care. *Make a point of finding out about them afterwards.*

If there are no victims requiring care and the problem cannot be fixed quickly, resume your speech and fight to overcome the problem. If the sound system has gone wrong, do without it – look towards the back of the hall and PROJECT YOUR MAGNIFICENT VOICE. If you cannot show the visual aids, do without them. As we shall see later on, no speech actually needs visual aids. A speaker always gets marks for determination.

If only you are aware of the emergency do not draw attention to it. Think quickly of a strategy to combat it. Previous speaker has taken your best points? Acknowledge this briefly and with a compliment ('As X has shown so clearly . . .') and then repeat the bare point(s) with no supporting material. Move on to another point in your speech.

If the event is overrunning you should have time to make instant cuts in your speech – begin with any surviving little darlings, and then start cutting from the middle – anything in the category of supporting material, anecdotes, jokes, facts other than killer facts. If you really run out of time cut your speech down to:

1. Thank yous.
2. Your three (at most) important points in one sentence with no supporting material.
3. Contact address for anyone in audience who wants to write to you.
4. Strong finish.
5. Do the job of your speech (urge audience to vote/present gold watch/open new building, etc.).

It is rare for a speech to become totally obsolete between composition and delivery but at times a speech may be ambushed by some unexpected event. If that happens, give yourself some thinking time. Decide whether any of the speech is salvageable – cut out the ruined sections and deliver the rest. If the speech is totally wrecked, scrawl some notes for a new one and talk about something else. If the audience know the title of your old speech, acknowledge and explain the change briefly, if they don't, don't.

If you accidentally cut some of your speech, do not restore it later in the wrong place. It is probably a sign that it was not worth saying. If you make a mistake on a matter of fact, correct it as soon as possible without an apology. If you make any other kind of mistake (say, mangling the punch line of a joke) ignore it. The chances are that no one noticed.

Heckles, interventions, questions

Some people are very accomplished public speakers when they are delivering their prepared speech, but go completely to pieces when they have to deal with someone else. There are three sources of outside interference for speakers, two permitted (interventions and questions), one not (heckling).

The golden rule for heckling is to ignore it. Tell the host in advance that you intend to do this and that you expect him or her to deal with rude or persistent hecklers before you continue speaking. If a heckler is genuinely witty and amused the audience, permit yourself a smile but do not respond. With any other sort of heckler, pause, make no acknowledgement or eye contact with him (it nearly always is 'him') and wait for the audience or the host to deal with him. At some social

The golden rule for heckling is to ignore it.

dinners, some bibulous members of the audience may feel they have the right to contribute to the after-dinner speeches. Even if you have a brilliant funny rejoinder, resist the temptation to use it. Speak to your whole audience, not just one person.

In certain kinds of structured debate (including the British Parliament and the US Congress) people can stand up and ask to intervene in your speech. They will make a quick point of their own, usually, by convention, in the form of a question. You do not have to accept these but it is better to take at least some of them, especially from your principal opponents. Do not fret about them. You have probably rehearsed them. It is very unlikely that an intervention will leave you dumbfounded: on the contrary, if you are speaking well and are on top of your subject they will give you a chance to shine and win over your audience. Do not accept an intervention in the middle of your best passages, but when you have completed them by all means pause and take an intervention then. You will be fighting your opponent on your strongest ground when you hope you have won the audience over. If the opponent who has been dying to intervene now declines the opportunity you have given him, then you will have made an effective point to the audience. Make certain they have seen your invitation and his refusal.

Do not take interventions within interventions. Finish dealing with one intervener before you take on another.

If you can rebut an intervention quickly, with a killer fact, do it. If you can rebut an intervention quickly, with a killer fact, do it. If it is right, accept it graciously, but cap it with a much more telling point of your own. Don't just say 'I'm coming to that point', even if you are. It always sounds weak. Try to anticipate very briefly what you are going to say about that point. In all cases, replay the intervention.

Begin your preparations for questions with the host. Establish with him or her clearly in advance whether and for how long you can expect questions. If you do not want to answer questions on your whole speech, tell the host that you want questions limited to certain parts.

Your plan, your actual writing and your rehearsals should have identified most of the likely questions and you should be able to answer them.

The golden rule for dealing with questions is to repeat them. Then deal with them honestly and at face value. Assume that even a loaded question is a genuine request for information and deal with it on that basis. However, you should not reply at all to questions which are personally insulting.

If you have the facts and information to reply to a question, present them logically and accurately. If you cannot answer a factual question, say so, promise to write to the questioner if he or she leaves a contact address with the host, and move on instantly to another questioner. Do *not* allow the questioner to supply the answer to his or her question because it is probably a killer fact against you.

Very often a 'questioner' will not even ask a question but make an impromptu speech. Don't stop this, it is your host's job and the impromptu speaker is making you look better to the audience and eating into time for difficult questions from someone else. If a question finally emerges, sum up the questioner's point very quickly (impressing your audience with the contrast between your well-organized mind and the questioner's rambling). Refute it with a killer fact if you have one, otherwise simply repeat your strongest point.

If you get no questions at all, try prompting the audience by asking something you want to answer: 'I am often asked . . .' You might even throw quick questions at them, with a Yes–No answer, or invite instant shows of hands.

Do *not* plant questions. They always get spotted and you will be discredited.

SUMMARY

- Brilliant speakers throughout history have suffered from stage fright.
- Recognize stage fright as normal and natural.
- You can use many physical and mental techniques to tackle particular symptoms of stage fright.
- With the right preparation you will not regard an audience as terrifying or powerful, and you will feel that they are lucky to have you.
- Don't rely on drugs to tackle stage fright.
- Good writing and thorough rehearsal will help you make the most of your voice, but you should also learn by experiment how to control and vary your breathing, pitch, pace and expression.
- Beware of all microphones.
- Stillness, pauses and eye contact are the most effective gestures. If you use other gestures, make them emphatic.
- It often helps to be a ham actor of yourself.
- In an emergency, adapt, cut or rewrite your speech. Do not apologize for coping with an emergency or a mistake.
- Ignore hecklers. Be prepared for interventions and questions.

13

Vision on

The use and abuse of visual aids

None of the great speakers in history have needed a visual aid. That includes you. If you have something worthwhile to say, if you write it clearly and expressively, and deliver it with variety and conviction you are all the visual aid which you need.

For many years one of Britain's most compelling speakers was the historian, A. J. P. Taylor. He built up a massive following on television – yet all he did was lecture straight to camera. The power of his thoughts and words was quite enough.

None of the great speakers in history have needed a visual aid. That includes you.

The basic point about all visual aids is that they should be the servants of your speech, not its master. The better the visual aids, the more risk that they will dictate the structure and content of the speech. The temptation is strongest with PowerPoint and its competitors, and I have listened to many speeches where the 'speaker' has just become an aural accompaniment to the slides.

An allied problem with visual aids is that they can actually limit your audience's imagination, and again, the better the visual aid, the higher the risk. People receive information in very different ways; they have unique personal translation systems of the words they hear from outside into data and ideas which they can use from inside. Some will translate them into a visual image, some will not, and for those that do, each visual image will be different.

To take a simple example, suppose that you mention a series of statistics: 10 per cent, 17 per cent, 35 per cent. Immediately you flash up a visual aid. The conventional wisdom is that percentages show up best with a pie chart, so you use an elegant, well-marked chart with all the right slices of pie. But not everyone in the audience sees percentages as pie slices. For some people percentages are jellybeans, 10 red, 17 yellow, 35 green. Others are more focused on the relationship of the percentages – they might mentally see a bar chart not a pie chart, with a 10-high bar and a 17-high bar and a towering 35-high bar. Still others assimilate percentages directly, with no visual cue. For all those impieous people the pie chart adds nothing to their understanding and may even impede it.

Another point about your audience is that many people, especially in academic settings, tape speeches. They cannot tape something visual.

There are more practical problems with visual aids. The most obvious is that they are visual. They make you learn another language, to do with colours and shapes and spatial relationships and symbols and icons and typography and what people can see at the back. Visual aids are about *adding* something to spoken words and you add nothing to spoken words just by displaying them. During the 1950s lots of low-budget sci-fi movies featured a scene in which the invariably male scientist would say to the female assistant: 'The only possible explanation is that we are being invaded by gamma-ray carrots from Mars.' She would gasp 'You mean? . . .' and he would say 'Yes, let me show you on the screen.' He would then switch on a screen showing the words GAMMA-RAY CARROTS MARS.

If you want to avoid this trap in your visual aids, you must become not only a writer but an illustrator.

All visual aids require extra preparation and expense and mastery of complex high-tech equipment such as a blackboard or flip-chart. (Drawing on a blackboard and exposing the right page in a flip-chart are expert skills.) They need setting up and rehearsal. If you hand something out for the audience to keep, you have to bring enough of them. If you hand something out for them to pass round and examine, you have to make sure that you get it back, and not broken or grubby. Visual aids are so many extra things to go wrong and to get anxious about.

For all these reasons it is very tempting to declare yourself an A. J. P. Taylor and do without them. However, used rightly, they are a valuable extra resource. They can make an audience remember the things you want remembered and they can give key passages a unique additional impact. In some circumstances a visual aid is more than an aid, it is actually integral to understanding a speech. If you are talking about an artist or an actor or a sportsperson you *need* illustrations of his or her work or him or her in action, about a movie or TV show you *need* clips from it, about a battle you *need* a battle-plan and almost certainly you will gain from a battle-plan in sequence. If you are talking about any sort of unfamiliar place, from eighteenth-century London to the planet Mercury, you certainly *need* a map and almost certainly you will gain from zooming in and out of detail.

In some cases, you may want or need an aural aid rather than a visual one. In a speech about music you may want to use tapes or possibly a piano or guitar. I would not advise you to compete against a live orchestra. There are other speeches where a sound cue might be appropriate (for example, an extract from a radio broadcast or an advertising jingle). Exactly the same principles apply as to visual aids.

If a visual aid has this much importance in your speech you need to incorporate it into all your planning and writing. If the aid is going to be permanently on view (say a map) you need to explain it early on.

The three Rs

If you decide to use visual aids or sound remember the three Rs. Be relevant. Be rational. Be ruthless.

Be relevant

Do not use any images or sound which are not totally integrated into your speech. Do not use any which might take attention away from your speech, which might make the audience think about, or worse still remember, things you did not intend to tell them. Do not use images and sounds for incidental entertainment.

Be rational

Use images or sounds which accurately convey the information you want your audience to have.

Be ruthless

Images and sound work best in small quantities. Use them very sparingly and shut them off the second they achieve their effect. Even if they are relevant and rational, do not use images or sounds which add nothing to the effect of your words. One of the most irritating features of television news is the pointless image, caused by the compulsion of television to illustrate. If there is a story about dairy farming, up comes the library footage of Daisy the Cow.

Now let us go back to Chapter 4 on Speech architecture, and look at the plan on page 36 for the speech on the Metropolitan Police.

```
1. Crime in London early C19th
   (a) high crime areas        V1 MAP LONDON 1825
   (b) social problems         V2 PRINT GIN DRINKER
   (c) organized crime         V3 PRINT BILL SYKES
2. Policing in London
   (d) private patrols
   (e) Peel in government       V4 CARTOON PEEL
   (f) Met Police founded 1829  V5 PRINT 'PEELER IN
                                UNIFORM'
```

The speaker lists five visual aids. The first one, the map of nineteenth-century London is relevant and informative. Since the speaker is likely to mention London places throughout the speech, the map should be permanently on view where the speaker can point to it. The second, the image of the gin drinker, will add nothing to the speaker's description of social problems in London and it will actually hinder the audience's memory of social problems other than alcohol. The third image – Dickens's Bill Sykes – will also add nothing to the words, and why make the audience think about a fictional criminal instead of a real one? The fourth image – Peel – is marginal. It is relevant and rational, and it may help the audience to remember a now obscure historical figure. But is he really needed? The police are the story, not Peel. The fifth image – an early Metropolitan policeman in uniform – is worth keeping. It will help the audience to understand and remember important information about the subject of the speech.

The three Rs have stripped out three unnecessary images, saved the speaker time and anxiety, and produced the maximum effect from the survivors.

The art of elimination

An effective visual aid conveys information accurately and without waste. An image achieves this not by what it shows but by what it leaves out. In a great work of art, every detail is part of the artist's plan, and anything not part of the plan is eliminated. You are a great artist and your approach should be the same.

The first thing to eliminate from any image is words. You are already using words in your speech. Your image should not need them. It should contain only the words needed to identify what the image is about – for example, labelling everything illustrated in a chart or diagram. (If you do not own the image you will also have to include identification of the copyright owner.) There is a very practical as well as a logical reason for eliminating words in an image. You want the audience to see them.

The first thing to eliminate from any image is words.

With this in mind, take it on trust from me that you have at most 25 words to play with in a visual aid. In a chart or diagram you will need most if not all of them for essential labelling of its individual components. If you have any words left over use them to deliver a key message rather than simply labelling the whole image. For example, instead of saying 'Exports by region 1999' you might say 'EU largest market in 1999'.

Having wiped out all unnecessary words, you must now eliminate any unnecessary image. Kill at once any cute little cartoon character or clip art. Eliminate your organization's logo. In a photograph crop any unnecessary detail. In a chart or diagram represent visually only the things you want to talk about. In the chart of Exports by region 1999 you might not want to represent all the world's regions. Perhaps the only significant ones in your speech are the EU, North America and the Far East. In that case, do not show the other regions at all, unless for some reason you are making a percentage comparison, in which case you can collapse all the rest into a single entry for Others.

A good visual aid will not be too crowded. People absorb visual information best when it stands out against blank space. For the same reason, eliminate any cutesy tricks with lettering, fonts, shadows, 3D effects, letters appearing and disappearing, and eliminate pointless, distracting colour and graphic effects. As we have noted, although a font with serifs is easier for you to read in manuscript, a sans-serif font is better for a visual aid.

A good visual aid will not be too crowded.

Types of visual aid

Here are a few notes on the strengths and weaknesses of different types of visual aids, in the approximate order of their invention. Every one of them needs careful planning and rehearsal to make it work at its best.

Maps (including hypothetical maps, battle plans, etc.)

- *Strengths*: genuine, often essential aid to understanding.
- *Potential weaknesses*: visibility of all details to all audience, zoom in for special features needs technology, if unfamiliar place needs clear indication of scale (not just numbers but comparator familiar to audience, e.g. New York to Washington DC).

Exhibit

A physical example, replica or model of the thing you are actually talking about (e.g. Aztec artefact, teddy bear, scale model of *Titanic*).

- *Strengths*: exceptional audience interest, accuracy of information.
- *Potential weaknesses*: if present constantly, may distract audience. May be hard to hold up exhibit and talk from notes/text at same time. May be hard for all audience to see exhibit which may need to be passed around, if so leave this until after your speech. If passed, risk of damage/theft. Tell audience which way you want it passed.

Photographs

A photograph has much the same *strengths* and *weaknesses* as an exhibit. It is interesting and accurate, but it may be hard to see and if it is permanently on view it may distract your audience from your speech. Unlike an exhibit, a photograph can be cropped and edited to remove extraneous details. This has been done so frequently in the modern age for faking and propaganda that you may feel slightly uncomfortable doing this yourself. If there is any chance that your audience might spot your editing (for example, because you are using a very familiar photograph) do not do it, because it will inspire mistrust.

Like all images, a photograph is potentially copyright. Check that you have the right to use it.

Diagram/chart/graph

- *Strengths*: can be made in advance. Diagram is excellent way to illustrate complex object or process. Rules and conventions of charts, if observed, can help most audiences absorb information by giving early indication of the type of information being conveyed, e.g. pie chart for percentages, bar chart for comparison of magnitudes, time moving from left to right on graph.

- *Potential weaknesses*: risk of clutter and irrelevant information, very hard for audience to take notes, risk of percentages not adding up to 100 per cent (will infuriate some audience members). Some audiences may not take in information through conventions.

Because charts and graphs are schematic there is a special need to make them transparent and honest. It is very easy to play tricks with scale, and slope and starting lines which can completely change the presentation of information; for example, you can make falling sales look like a small, temporary blip (if you are the CEO) or a dramatic plunge (if you are an angry shareholder). If anyone in your audience spots that you have used a specious presentation in a chart or a graph it will inspire mistrust in you and your speech.

Slides

High-quality slides have more impact than photographs, but of course they require a projector and a darkened room and Murphy's familiar law will ensure that at least some of them will be in the wrong order or upside down. Slides are no help to audience members who want to tape your speech or even take notes. They also automatically slow down your speech and risk taking it over altogether (see Photographs).

Blackboard (plus modern counterpart the felt tip board)

- *Strengths*: easy to use (felt tip more than blackboard), nothing to go wrong, you can add and subtract during speech, create simple, memorable information, create automatic suspense for audience as they wonder what you are writing, allow audience time to catch up on notes.
- *Potential weaknesses*: they take time (reduce this by putting diagrams/sketch plans, etc. on board in advance and write only words during speech), may be hard to read for audiences (yellow chalk on green board is easiest), chalk and pens may squeak horribly, your awful handwriting, your poor spelling.

Flip chart

- *Strengths* Much as for blackboard and felt board. Can be prepared in advance, but still amended during speech, an effective way to convey simple, memorable information, especially good for any kind of process, automatic suspense and drama (what's under the blank page?), allows audience to take notes.
- *Potential weaknesses*: can be hard to see, especially for those at the back (help them by leaving bottom third blank on each page), risk of over-detail (limit bullet points to three per page), tearing too many pages or wrecking a page (you will have to learn the expert 'matador tear', a short, sharp tug at the corner). If you write, again you risk exposing your awful handwriting and speling.

Writing on a flip chart needs to be at least 1.25 inches (3.5 cm) high and even bigger if anyone is more than 30 feet (9.1 metres) away. This gives you terribly few words to play with, even with the big page. Use bold colours not pastels, but remember that by convention red still implies emphasis. Do not use ONLY UPPER CASE LETTERS.

If you are using a blackboard or felt board or flip chart, do not talk while you are writing and have your back to the audience. When you want to point to it, do not point across your body (i.e. use your nearest hand to the board).

Audiotape

- *Strengths*: obviously essential if you need to convey aural information, always dramatic and interesting for audience, allows time for note taking.
- *Potential weaknesses*: needs reliable equipment, sound system. It is surprisingly easy to forget to introduce an audio section properly and suddenly switch on the tape. And obviously, you have to stop speaking and stand or sit still.

Film, video clips

- *Strengths*: drama, audience interest, accuracy.
- *Potential weaknesses*: need equipment and darkened room. Stop your speech dead and may overshadow it.

Overhead projector

- *Strengths*: versatile and accurate – can project anything which can be copied (but watch out for copyright). Easy to prepare transparencies in advance and add to them in speech. Parts can be hidden by card for suspense. Transparencies can be laid on top of each other to show progress or add complexity. Can be used in lighted room, by speaker facing audience at all times.
- *Potential weaknesses*: temperamental projectors, dust, bad focus. Visibility. (Needs more rehearsal than any other medium.) Too many words, cluttered details on transparencies. Too many transparencies overshadowing speaker, leaving transparency projected too long distracting audience.

Powerpoint (and competitors)

Powerpoint is a Microsoft software presentation package which you can use to create original material in almost any medium, using both images and sound. It carries a big stock of clip art, images, fonts, letters, colours and effects but will also accept any internet or computer-generated material. It will accept movie images and will allow you to create animations and special effects. You can amend and re-amend your material. When you are finally satisfied with it, you can display this material on a computer or a projection system, disseminate it through the internet and convert it to print.

- *Strengths*: accuracy, impact and astonishing versatility.

- *Potential weaknesses*: simply too good and too easy. Too tempting to create amazing effects or simply too many slides and forget to write a decent speech. May simply take over audience's attention.

Handouts

Handouts can be prepared in advance and can convey information to your audience in a lasting way. A handout may be anything from a book to a business card.

The golden rule about handouts is not to hand them out until you have finished speaking. An audience will always look at a handout in preference to listening to you – it is simply human nature. And if your handout is too informative the ruder members of your audience will walk away with it and have a drink.

There are a few exceptions to the principle of handing nothing out until after the speech. If you are going to be referring constantly to something in your speech (a map or one particular text) you may want to give it out in advance. If despite all your careful planning your speech has an exceptionally complex structure you may want to hand out a simplified plan of your speech to help the audience work out where you are. (In that case you must stick to that structure.)

Finally, you may sometimes want to hand out a full copy of your speech in advance to members of the media. If your speech is long it is a courtesy to journalists who may have tight deadlines and will help you to be reported. If you do this, you must add the words **Check against delivery** to the heading, and include an embargo **NOT FOR PUBLICATION BEFORE** . . . the speech has finished.

Make certain there are enough handouts to go round. Audience members react like children at a birthday party if they miss a handout.

SUMMARY

- Visual and aural aids are never necessary, but used well they can enrich your speech and make your key points memorable.
- Visual and aural aids should be the servants of your speech not its master.
- Words are no better just for being displayed on a screen.
- Visual and aural aids have different strengths, weaknesses and technical demands, but they all need careful planning and rehearsal. If you are planning to use any of them, make certain that your setting has the right equipment for them.
- Be relevant, rational and ruthless in your use of visual and aural aids.
- Keep visual aids sparse and simple. Eliminate all unnecessary words and detail.
- Hand out no handout until you have finished speaking. Make certain there are enough to go round.

Speaking to the world

Using the media, publishing your speech

A public speech should reach the widest possible public. Your marvellous thoughts and words should go out to the world, not just the audience in the hall. That means using the media to get immediate publicity for your speech and in the longer term it may mean getting your speech published, in whole or in part.

Using the media

In Chapters 1 and 4, we have already talked about the demands which the media can make in the preparation of your speech and the conduct of the occasion, and how they can conflict with the needs of the live audience.

Give the media nothing else to report but your speech.

You must decide whether you want to meet those demands. If it is essential for you to be reported instantly you really have no choice. If you want the media present you must agree this with the host organization for your speech, and then agree (or take charge of) the arrangements for them. Do *not* agree to speak until you are satisfied with these arrangements. Obviously, this is not a problem if your own organization is in charge of the speech occasion.

You must make an advance decision on whether you will take questions from the media after your speech or whether you will give them interviews. I would advise against either, because you will lose control of the agenda and you allow the media to pick the story they are going to write or broadcast. What is the point of writing such a brilliant speech if it is not going to be the story? Give the media nothing else to report but your speech.

As we have said earlier you do not have to take questions at all, but if you do it is quite legitimate and a sound precaution to limit questions to members of the audience, not the media, and to the subject of your speech.

There is another major reason for refusing interviews after a speech. Delivering a live speech generates a great deal of emotion and energy. When you have finished you will probably feel exhausted and exhilarated at the same time. This is altogether the wrong condition for media interviews, when you need to be calm and alert. It is even more dangerous to relax with a few drinks with your friends in the media. You are even more likely to blurt something which takes the entire story away from your speech. (Interviews and friendly drinks can be even more dangerous if you are the speech-writer, not the speaker. You will be just as exhausted and exhilarated as your speaker, but you will also be flattered to be interviewed or to be asked to join the bantering circle of journos at the bar. The most stupid things I ever said as a speech-writer were blurted in those circumstances, and when I switched to being a political journalist I always targeted a politician's hired help.)

If you are on a publicity tour or any sort of campaign you cannot afford to turn interviews away. But do them before your speech, not after, and do not let them interfere with your practical or mental preparations for the speech. You will want to keep these interviews focused on the subject of your speech without giving too much of it away in advance. Check when the interview is being broadcast or published: if this is before your speech, try to give 'teasers' for what you are going to say rather than delivering the actual content. 'In my speech tonight, Ann, I am going to explain why the American bee is in danger of extinction and what we need to do right away to fight bee disease . . .'

Make sure that you include local and specialist media in any interviews you give and be briefed on their concerns. Local and specialist media are in general more likely to give you coverage and less likely to be hostile. Moreover, although they have a smaller reach of readers and listeners than national media they are more likely to be trusted and believed by their followers.

I suggested earlier that you should try to keep the media focused on your speech and nothing else. However, at times you may actually want to take the opportunity to initiate or respond to another story as well. You may feel that you have no choice: there may be an ongoing media story, not covered in your speech, and it would be unrealistic or dangerous to ignore it. In those circumstances you may be tempted to give an interview about it. Resist the temptation, even if you are a very experienced interviewer. Uncouple that other story from your speech. Prepare a separate statement on that story, have it issued from somewhere else, and decline any questions or interviews on that story from the journalists covering the speech.

If you decide on this strategy for using the media, make sure that everyone concerned is aware that you want to concentrate exclusively on your speech. In fact, whatever media strategy you choose, make everyone stick to it. That means not only your own organization's staff and media people but also your host organization. Do not let any well-intentioned members try to act as spin-doctors on your behalf. Do not let anyone but yourself or your staff answer questions about your speech. Do not assume that just because a host organization is friendly it is safe to talk about sensitive issues to its members in a private setting. They may get leaked to the media. For the same reason do not get drunk or stoned after your speech, or make a pass at anyone. It is easy to do these things in the after-glow of a big speech. Whether you are the speaker or the speech-writer, your job is certainly not over when the speech is finished. Do not do any wild celebrations until the speech is safely reported.

Do not get drunk or stoned after your speech, or make a pass at anyone.

The art of the press release

You can always release the full text of your speech. If the speech is important and has to go on the record, you may have no choice. As mentioned earlier, it is a courtesy to the media to release a long speech a little time before you deliver it: remember to say **Check against delivery** and to include an embargo.

Even if you release the full text it is worth preparing a press release, summarizing the key points of your speech *in the way that you would like them reported*. For this reason, you must compose and issue your press release yourself: do *not* allow the host organization, however friendly, the chance to edit your words and message.

The full text of a speech allows the media to pick and choose what they report from it. That is one reason why it is so risky to use irony in a speech: it can and will be reported as if you meant it. In fact before releasing the full text of any speech you should have it edited *all over again* because the text will now be doing a quite different job. The editor should look for any phrase at all which could be quoted out of context, and if necessary, rewrite it to make it impossible for it to be misinterpreted. This might well mean cutting or rewriting a little darling. A historic example was the British Prime Minister Harold Macmillan who became famous in the mid-1950s for boasting to the British people 'you've never had it so good'. He actually said 'most of our people have never had it so good', and the surrounding text makes clear that he was not boasting at all, but warning that prosperity might not last. Macmillan is now remembered inaccurately for the boast, not the warning. An edited text might have saved his reputation. It might have said 'Although most of our people have never had it so good, it may not be this good for ever.'

Before releasing the full text of any speech you should have it edited *all over again*.

If you use a press release, you shut down the opportunities for the media to misinterpret your speech. You have an excellent chance to get your speech reported your way, because it is far easier for any reporter to use your press release rather than read your full text, still less listen to it and make notes.

The key to a successful press release is to make it a complete story, that is, to make it possible to report your speech in print or on air without going to any other source. It should be composed to allow an abbreviated but accurate story of the speech to be conveyed *in the first two paragraphs* of text.

A press release should open by identifying itself as a press release, and indicate when it can be used, either **For immediate release** or **For release at** [give a date and time in 24-hour clock].

The next step is to identify **the speaker** and deliver a headline message.

Then add the setting and time for the speech, repeat **the speaker's name** and status and end with the word 'said': followed by the headline message in the form of a direct quotation. Then use two paragraphs to tell the basic story of the speech in indirect quotation.

Now you may use most, but not all, of the rest of the page to give a longer story of the speech, in *descending* order of importance (sub-editors in a hurry always cut from the bottom). Most of this will be in indirect quotation, but you may quote yourself directly where you think you have been concise and memorable. You may edit your actual words slightly to manufacture a direct quotation. For example, Winston Churchill once said: 'I cannot forecast to you the action of Russia. It is a riddle wrapped in a mystery inside an enigma; but perhaps there is a key. That key is Russian national interest.' In a press release he might reasonably have compressed this to: 'The action of Russia is a riddle wrapped in a mystery inside an enigma. But the key is Russian national interest.'

If you want key facts to be remembered, make them stand out as bullet points on the press release. However do not end a press release with a bullet point, but use a full paragraph, of either direct or indirect speech.

When you have finished put in italics below the final text the word *ends*. If you absolutely must continue onto another page put instead of *ends* the words *more follows* or *mf.* Or you may put a slash / followed by the first significant words of the next paragraph as in /The policy of the opposition . . .

After *ends* you must give a contact number for more information and indicate where, if possible, any reporter can obtain the full text of the speech.

You may then choose to give any further relevant information about the speaker, the setting, the host organization, the background to the event, preceded by the words NOTES FOR EDITORS.

A model press release in this form is shown as an example. (The facts mentioned are correct.)

For release at 20:30 Monday 31 June 2003

[after speaker has finished but in time for late news bulletins, most overnight editions]

For all media *from Frances Catt, MP (Purrgressive party) for Market Snodsbury*

Catt: *'Immigrants are more valuable to our country than North Sea Oil.'*

Delivering the Dogberry Memorial Lecture in the Percy Jeeves Hall, Market Snodsbury, Woostershire, at 7.30 pm on 31 June 2003 (Monday), Frances Catt MP urged the government to 'correct the poisonous lies about immigrants from stupid, vicious sections of the media'. She called for a national education campaign on the benefits of immigration.

Ms Catt said: 'Immigrants contribute seven times more to the UK economy than North Sea Oil. Their output is worth around £1,600 for every man, woman, and child in this country.' Immigrants pay more tax than they receive in state benefits. Without them, the standard rate of income tax would have to rise by at least 1p.

Quoting official figures from a recent Home Office study on immigration Ms Catt said immigrants were an essential part of Britain's labour force

- 31 per cent of all Britain's doctors
- 15 per cent of all Britain's natural scientists
- one-eighth of all Britain's academic and research staff
- one in seven of all Britain's transport workers

were born outside Britain.

Ms Catt said that immigrants would be even more important in Britain's future. In the next 25 years, we actually need *more* immigrants to replenish the population and provide for the growing proportion of retired people. Without immigrants our health service and our pension system will be bankrupt before 2030 and our old people will be destitute.

'Throughout our history our country has always benefited from immigration and always resented immigrants. Each new wave of immigrants has faced its own wave of fear and hatred from the native population, before being accepted for the gifts they brought to our country. I urge the government to break this vicious cycle by a national education campaign.' *Ends*

All inquiries to Jean Le Souris, Press Office **+44 (0)20 7xxx xxxx**

Full text of speech available at **www.cattnmouse.parl.uk**

Notes for editors

Frances Catt was first elected MP for Market Snodsbury in 1983.

The Dogberry Memorial Lecture was founded in 1974 and is given each year in Market Snodsbury on a topic which is relevant to community policing. Previous speakers include Sir Augustus Fink-Nottle OM FRS, Nobel Prize Winner for his work on newts, novelist Rosie M. Banks and her husband Archbishop Bing O'Little.

The Home Office study is called *Migration: An Economic and Social Analysis* and was published by The Stationery Office in January 2002.

Publishing your speech

Any speech is worth publishing, in full or in part. Some newspapers and journals regularly publish extracts from speeches but it is more likely that you will have to edit it into an article. It may also be a chapter in a book. If you decide on a book, do not simply collect your speeches and smack them down side by side. Instead, rewrite them and update them, and then edit them into a coherent, flowing scheme of chapters. A book needs footnotes to identify sources of facts and quotations. Of course you kept these carefully in the final edit of your speech, didn't you?

Any speech is worth publishing, in full or in part.

If your host organization or other bodies ask to publish your speech, insist on viewing what they intend to publish. Do not let a hostile organization or individual publish your words if you think they would be distorted. Remember that the copyright on them belongs to you or your organization. Threaten the 'enemy' if they breach copyright by quoting them extensively.

SUMMARY

- Establish with your host the media arrangements you want for your speech.

- It is nearly always a good idea to focus the media exclusively on your speech and not to give interviews after your speech at which other issues may be raised.

- Even if you release the full text of your speech, compose and issue a summary in a press release.

- Let your press release tell a complete story of your speech the way you want it told.

- Keep control of the publication of your speech.

Appendix

Some high impact speeches – and what makes them work

In this appendix I have set out some speeches, or extracts from speeches, from different times and in different settings and suggested what makes them work. Before any analysis, read each one out aloud. Feel free to disagree with my choices or my analysis.

Queen Elizabeth I: 'The Golden Speech' November 1601

The Queen had reigned for 44 years and was 69, lonely and exhausted, when she summoned her energies to make this speech, which for generations was remembered as a model of perfection. It was delivered to kneeling members of her House of Commons. Underneath its majestic prose, it is an astute politician's speech – by a politician with fences to mend. Her country was fighting a long, profitless war against Spain, the economy was depressed and the House of Commons had many financial grievances against the Queen's government. The Queen spends a long time connecting with her audience before disconnecting herself from her unpopular ministers. I have condensed one passage, and amended some spellings and punctuation to a modern style.

"Mr Speaker, we perceive your coming is to present thanks unto us. Know that I accept them with no less joy than your loves can have desire to offer such a present, and do more esteem it than any treasure or riches. For those we know how to prize, but loyalty, love and thanks, I account them invaluable (1); and though God hath raised me high, yet this I account the glory of my crown, that I have reigned with your loves. (2) This makes that I do not so much rejoice that God hath made me to be a queen, as to be a queen over so thankful a people, and to be the means under God to conserve you in safety and preserve you from danger, yea to be the instrument to deliver you from dishonour,

from shame, and from infamy, to keep you from cruel servitude, and from slavery under our enemies *(3)* and cruel tyranny, and vile oppression intended against us, for the better understanding whereof we take very acceptable their intended helps, and chiefly in that it manifesteth your loves and largeness of hearts to your sovereign. Of myself I must say this, I was never any greedy scraping grasper *(4)*, nor a strict fast-holding prince, nor yet a waster, my heart was never set upon any worldly goods, but only for my subjects' good. What you do bestow on me I will not hoard up, but receive it to bestow on you again; yea mine own properties I account yours to be expended for your good *(5)*, and your eyes shall see the bestowing of it for your welfare.

Mr Speaker, I would wish you and the rest to stand up, for I fear I shall yet trouble you with longer speech *(6)*.

Mr Speaker, you give me thanks, but I am more to thank you, and I charge you thank them of the Lower House from me, for had I not received knowledge from you, I might have fallen into the lapse of an error only for want of true information.

Since I was Queen, yet did I never put my pen to any grant but upon pretext and semblance made me that it was for the good and avail of my subjects generally, though a private profit to some of my ancient servants who have deserved well; but that my grants shall be made grievances to my people and oppressions, to be privileged under colour of our patents *(7)*, our princely dignity shall not suffer it.

When I heard it, I could give no rest unto my thoughts until I had reformed it, and those varlets, lewd persons, abusers of my bounty *(8)* shall know I will not suffer it. *The Queen then thanked the Speaker and the Commons for raising their grievances and said again that her people's love was her highest value.*

In my governing this land, I have ever set the last judgment day before mine eyes, and so to rule I shall be judged and answer before a higher Judge, to whose judgment seat I do appeal *(9)*: in that never thought was cherished in my heart that tended not to my people's good.

And if my princely bounty have been abused; and my grants turned to the hurt of my people contrary to my will and meaning, or if any in authority under me have neglected or converted what I have committed unto them, I hope God will not lay their culps to my charge.

To be a king and wear a crown is a thing more glorious to them that see it than it's pleasant to them that bear it *(10)*; for myself I never was so much enticed with the glorious name of a king, or the royal authority of a queen, as delighted that God hath made me his instrument to maintain his truth and glory, and to defend this kingdom from dishonour, damage, tyranny and oppression. But should I ascribe any of these things to myself or my sexly weakness, I were not worthy to live, and of all most unworthy of the mercies I have received at God's hands, but to God only and wholly all is given and ascribed. *(11)*

The cares and troubles of a crown I cannot more fitly resemble than to the drugs of a learned physician, perfumed with some aromatical savour, or to bitter pills gilded over, by which they are made more acceptable or less offensive, which indeed are bitter and unpleasant to take *(12)*; and for my own part, were it not for conscience sake to discharge the duty that God hath laid upon me, and to maintain his glory, and keep you in safety, in mine own disposition I should be willing to resign the place I hold to any other, and glad to be freed of the glory with the labours, for it is not my desire to live nor to reign longer than my life and reign shall be for your good. And though you have had and may have many mightier and wiser princes sitting in this seat, yet you never had nor shall have any that will love you better.

Thus, Mr Speaker, I commend me to your loyal loves and yours to my best care and your further councils, and I pray you Mr Controller, and you of my council, that before these gentlemen depart into their countries, you bring them all to kiss my hand. *(13)*"

(1) She uses a trio of simple memorable words, followed by an anacoluthon, a deliberate change of construction to make her audience stop and think about her message.

(2) The key theme of her speech, in which the word 'love' is repeated frequently.

(3) A direct reminder of a common foe . . . The audience would have identified not only the external enemy, the Spaniards, but also the 'enemy within', the Catholic conspirators who inspired fear and dread which was far above their actual capability. Parliament was always urging the Queen to get tougher with the Catholics.

(4) In this stately language, she suddenly introduces a very down-to-earth image, made even more effective by alliteration. Winston Churchill often used the same surprise.

(5) A touch of hyperbole.

(6) A courteous gesture to the kneeling members, but also a very controlling one. She is virtually ordering them to pay attention.

(7) Having bathed her audience in mutual love, she is now addressing their specific grievance – the financial privileges she had given to favourites.

(8) The former favourites are quickly turned into another common foe.

(9) Perhaps a little late in the speech, she occupies the common ground between her and her audience, including her critics, that they are all subjects of God.

(10) A simple and memorable antithesis.

(11) There are many pairs of words in the speech but this double pair is especially rhythmic, helped by the inversion at the end of the sentence.

(12) A sustained metaphor – the monarchy a bitter pill made more palatable with aromas or gilding – which would have been especially vivid to her audience, since most contemporary medicines were horrid.

(13) This must have been a poignant moment – most of the audience would not have expected to see the Queen again. She died just over a year later.

John Donne: from a sermon on Mercy, Christmas Day 1624

John Donne (1572–1631) was one of England's greatest poets, who later entered the Church of England and became Dean of St Paul's. He was an immensely popular preacher, not only through his literary and dramatic gifts but because his sermons lasted for 45 minutes instead of the usual two to three hours. This passage ascends into poetry through simple rhythmic language, sustained, vivid and accurate analogies, and controlled changes of pace. I have changed some of the original punctuation to a modern style.

"God made sun and moon to distinguish seasons, and day and night, and we cannot have the fruits of the earth but in their seasons. But God hath made no decree to distinguish the seasons of his mercies. In paradise the fruits were ripe the first minute, and in heaven it is always autumn, his mercies are ever in their maturity. *(1)*

We ask *panem quotidianum,* our daily bread, and God never says you should have come yesterday, he never says you must again tomorrow but 'today if you will hear his voice', today he will hear you. *(2)*

If some king of the earth have so large an extent of dominion in north and south that he hath winter and summer together in his dominions, so large an extent east and west, as that he hath day and night together in his dominions, much more hath God mercy and judgment together. He brought light out of darkness, not out of a lesser light; He can bring thy summer out of winter, though thou have no spring: though in the ways of fortune or understanding or conscience, thou have been benighted till now, wintered and frozen, clouded and eclipsed, damped and benumbed, smothered and stupefied till now, now God comes to thee, *(3)* not as in the dawning of the day, not as in the bud of the spring, but as the sun at noon to illustrate all shadows, as the sheaves in harvest to fill all penuries: all occasions invite his mercies, and all times are his seasons."

(1) The image of perpetually ripe fruit would have been even more vivid in seventeenth-century England, which was full of orchards and where all plants had specific seasons.

(2) 'Today if you will hear his voice' is from Psalm 95 verse 7. Donne gives this biblical quotation importance by making it the climax of a trio.

(3) After the gathering pace of the pairs of words, Donne slows down to emphasize five simple but vital words.

Lincoln's Gettysburg Address 1863

Although it is at the top of most lists of the greatest speeches in history, Lincoln's Gettysburg Address was by no means the principal attraction for its original listeners. They gathered to hear the main speaker, Senator Everett, deliver a florid two-hour-long address parading classical learning and elaborate rhetorical devices. If you are interested, search for Everett's text on the internet and read as much as you can stand. Everett had the grace to congratulate Lincoln and prophesied, correctly, that his brief 'after-word' would be remembered. It illustrates almost every principle of great speech-writing.

"Fellow countrymen. (1) Four score and seven years ago, (2) our fathers brought forth on this continent a new nation, conceived in liberty and dedicated to the proposition that all men are created equal. (3)

Now we are engaged in a great civil war, testing whether that nation – or any nation so conceived and so dedicated (4) – can long endure. We are met on a great battlefield of that war. We have come to dedicate a portion of that field as a final resting-place for those who here gave their lives that that nation might live. It is altogether fit and proper that we should do this. (5)

But, in a larger sense, we cannot dedicate, we cannot consecrate, we cannot hallow this ground. (6) The brave men, living and dead, who struggled here have consecrated it far above our poor power to add

or detract. The world will little note nor long remember *(7)* what we say here, but it can never forget what they did here. *(8)* It is for us, the living, rather, to be dedicated here to the unfinished work which they who fought here have thus far so nobly advanced. *(9)* It is rather for us to be here dedicated to the great task remaining before us: that from these honoured dead we take increased devotion to that cause for which they gave the last full measure of devotion; that we here highly resolve that these dead shall not have died in vain; that this nation, under God, shall have a new birth of freedom – and that government of the people, by the people, for the people shall not perish from the earth. *(10)*"

(1) Lincoln immediately talks to his audience – unlike Everett who talked endlessly about himself. Today we use more inclusive language, but in those days women tolerated being called countrymen.

(2) Four score and seven might sound stilted, why not 87? But it is the language of the Bible, then and probably now the best-known book in the United States. Lincoln was invoking its authority and connecting with his audience through a familiar echo.

(3) Lincoln speaks briskly, stating something controversial as historic fact and giving the audience no time to think about it. At least half the dead at Gettysburg were fighting *against* the proposition that all men are created equal. Many of his live audience would also have disagreed with that idea.

(4) An echo – repeats words conceived and dedicated to remind people of big ideas behind them (liberty and equality).

(5) After a controversial opening remark, Lincoln reunites himself with all his audience, establishing, in this case quite literally, the common ground between them, and congratulating them all on their fit and proper purpose.

(6) Lincoln uses a trio – audiences remember ideas when they are put in threes. He wants the audience to remember this section because it has a big surprise (we are not dedicating this ground after all) and it is

introducing the big idea of the speech. Although there are no jokes in the speech, this passage is quite playful – a change of mood amidst solemnity.

(7) Beautiful pair 'little note nor long remember' and

(8) a strong antithesis 'we say here' against 'they did here'.

(9) 'It is for us the living . . .' He has cleared up the mystery of why we cannot dedicate the ground. Mystery is a good device for creating suspense and interest but Lincoln does not let it go on too long.

(10) Government of the people . . . Two bits of technique in one phrase – a repeat and a trio, create a memorable climax. The trio makes the audience remember what he is saying, the repeat of 'the people' makes them listen to the vital words before 'of . . . by . . . and for . . .' Those tiny words are carrying the big message – we are fighting for democracy.

There are 269 words in the Gettysburg address, nearly all of them short. Within that short space, there is a varied sentence structure and changes of mood and rhythm. Lincoln delivers an enormous message – the North must win for the sake of freedom and democracy – but he is still faithful to the stated purpose of speech, of dedication to the memory of the dead. Finally, there is no I in the speech, only we.

Susan B. Anthony: defence against an indictment for the criminal offence of voting in the US presidential election of 1872

Susan B. Anthony (1820–1906) was the leading American campaigner for votes for women. Faced with a $100 fine (the equivalent of over $1,400 today) for unlawfully voting her defence (which I have slightly edited and repunctuated) is a journey of inescapable logic, beginning from the 'common ground' of the American constitution.

"Friends and fellow-citizens: I stand before you tonight under indictment for the alleged crime of having voted at the last presidential election, without having a lawful right to vote. It shall be my work this evening to prove to you that in thus voting, I not only committed no crime but instead simply exercised my citizen's rights, guaranteed to me and all United States citizens by the National Constitution, beyond the power of any State to deny.

The preamble of the Federal constitution says: 'We the people of the United States, in order to form a more perfect union, establish justice, insure domestic tranquillity, provide for the common defense, promote the general welfare, and secure the blessings of liberty to ourselves and our posterity, do ordain and establish this Constitution for the United States of America.'

It was 'we the people', not 'we the white male citizens'; nor yet 'we, the male citizens', but we, the whole people, who formed the Union. And we formed it, not to give the blessings of liberty but to secure them, not to the half of ourselves and the half of our posterity but to the whole people – women as well as men. And it is a downright mockery to talk to women of their enjoyment of the blessings of liberty while they are denied the use of the only means of securing them provided by this democratic-republican government – the ballot.

For any state to make sex a qualification that must ever result in the disfranchisement of one entire half of the people is to pass a bill of attainder, or an *ex post facto* law, and is therefore a violation of the supreme law of the land. By it the blessings of liberty are for ever withheld from women and their female posterity. To them this government has no just powers derived from the consent of the governed. To them this government is not a democracy. It is not a republic. It is an odious aristocracy, a hateful oligarchy of sex, the most hateful aristocracy ever established on the face of the globe (1) . . .

Webster, Worcester and Bouvier (2) all define a citizen to be a person in the United States, entitled to vote and hold office.

The only question left to be settled now is: are women persons? And I hardly believe any of our opponents will have the hardihood to say they are not. Being persons, then, women are citizens; and no state has a right to make any law, or to enforce any old law, that shall abridge their privileges or immunities. Hence, every discrimination against women in the Constitutions and laws of the several states is today null and void, precisely as is every one against Negroes. *(3)*"

(1) A pair of Hooray! words (democracy, republic) contrasted with two Boo! words, to any American audience – aristocracy, oligarchy.

(2) All dictionaries and authorities.

(3) She was speaking in a Northern state which had only recently won the Civil War to strike down discrimination against Negroes. During the post-war era of Reconstruction many Northern (male) politicians railed against Southern aristocracy and resisted their efforts to prevent freed slaves from voting. Her conclusion was a clear invitation for the same politicians to give the same treatment to women.

Rt Hon. Denis Healey MP caricatures two Conservative prime ministers in 1991

My former employer, Denis Healey, had a gift for sustained insulting comic similes and metaphors. He famously likened an attack on him by his Conservative opponent, Geoffrey Howe, to being 'savaged by a dead sheep' and he exploited variations on the image for many years afterwards. The Healey analogies worked because they were accurate. In the House of Commons on 26 June 1991 he used the gift to caricature the new Conservative Prime Minister John Major and his predecessor Margaret Thatcher. For convenience I have edited out the conventional British parliamentary circumlocutions.

"Let me say a word about the Prime Minister. I watched his face as his predecessor spoke this afternoon and I have never seen such inspissated gloom etched on a human visage in my life. *(1)* When Mrs

Thatcher said that she planned to support him in the next election, he must have been reminded of Lenin's promise to support the social democrats as the rope supports the hanged man.

All of us like the Prime Minister and it is difficult to be rude about him – I have not attempted it *(2)* – but I must confess that he reminds me of one of the most notable characters in current folklore – Charlie Brown in 'Peanuts'. You may remember, Mr Speaker, because I am sure that you are an avid follower of 'Peanuts' *(3)*, that Charlie Brown was once approached by Lucy – a bossy little girl. *[Laughter]* The parallel escapes me *(4)*. Lucy asked Charlie to join her on an ocean cruise, so they got on the boat and she took Charlie up to the sun deck and said to Charlie 'Now Charlie, there you will see a stack of deckchairs, and you have to put your deckchair up – and Charlie, if you want to look backwards, you put it facing the stern of the boat' – which she obviously preferred herself – 'but if you want to look forward into the future, you place it facing the prow of the boat. Now Charlie,' she said, 'which way do you want your deckchair facing?' Charlie replied, so much like the Prime Minister, 'I don't seem able to get my deckchair unfolded.'

I hope, without great confidence, that the Prime Minister will manage to get his deckchair unfolded at some time in the next 12 months. But of course, after 12 months, the liner will be under a different captain. *(5)*"

(1) He makes his already receptive audience linger over his point with elaborate language, including the superbly expressive word 'inspissated'.

(2) But he is very clearly about to . . .

(3) The then Speaker, Bernard Weatherill, had a somewhat staid reputation and was an unlikely candidate as a fan of 'Peanuts'.

(4) Fake innocence – reproaching the audience for interpreting a remark as the speaker intended – is a reliable comic effect. Two great British comedians were famous exponents – Max Miller and Frankie Howerd. Both traded heavily on sexual innuendo and were always indignant that the audience took their material the wrong way. Howerd especially would

go into paroxysms of denial 'Oh no, no missus, no really, no, you should be ashamed . . .'

(5)   A general election was due, which John Major was expected to lose. Denis Healey neatly concludes the long comic excursion. But 'Charlie Brown' got his revenge by winning the election.

Healey's far-fetched analogy worked because it was accurate. Margaret Thatcher was a decisive, bossy Prime Minister, John Major always had trouble defining his premiership in her long shadow.

Alfred C. Decrane, Jr, 'Cheaper by the Gallon' 1995

Alfred C. Decrane, Jr was then chairman of the board of Texaco Inc. This is a slightly edited version of a speech delivered to the Executives' Club of Chicago on 17 November 1995. It is a model of how to present the case for a controversial industry and convey complex, technical information. Although Mr Decrane's business audience would have been largely sympathetic he had plenty of 'invisible opponents' (see Chapter 9) to deal with – consumers who thought the petroleum industry greedy, environmentalists who thought it irresponsible and exploitative in the Third World, and some anonymous experts. Mr Decrane meets these invisible opponents on their own ground – arguing with facts that his industry has been innovative and beneficial to consumers, the environment and the Third World.

"Thank you very much. Perhaps the title of my remarks surprises some of you? I chose it as a way to focus our attention on how the petroleum industry has met the challenge of keeping the world supplied with clean, affordable and plentiful energy – energy that's cheaper by the gallon. (1)

Today, on the streets of Chicago, a gallon of gasoline, including all taxes, costs about $1.40. Now some of you may feel that's too much. But factoring in inflation, taxes included, the retail price of gasoline

in the United States is nearly as low as it has ever been, since record keeping began in the 1920s.

It's cheaper than it was back in the early 70s, before the first Middle East oil embargo which more than quadrupled the price of crude oil. And it's even cheaper than the $2.00 or more we put out for a gallon of Coca-Cola or the $7.00 a gallon for Perrier water. (2)

Now, think back to that mid-70 period. In the wake of that first Mid-East oil embargo, this country was in shock. The embargo cost half a million Americans their jobs; US GNP fell by $50 billion; and America's sense of security faltered.

At the time, many alleged experts predicted crude oil prices would rise to $50 or $60 a barrel and beyond. Others claimed world oil reserves would dry up within 50 years. As they saw it, petroleum couldn't maintain its primacy as the world's economic, plentiful, fuel of choice.

Well, they were wrong (thank goodness for experts). (3)

Today:

- Oil and natural gas provide fully 60 per cent of the world's energy.

- Oil is selling for about $17 a barrel.

- Global reserves have been increased by 60 per cent even though worldwide consumption of hydrocarbons has risen 36 per cent during this period. (4)

Today, with oil consumption at about 70 million barrels per day, the world still has about a 50-year supply – and we continue to add to our reserve base.

How did that happen? The petroleum industry – through better management, innovation and technology – made it happen. It certainly wasn't luck.

Even if you've only followed the industry through the occasional news piece, you know we are leaner, more streamlined; with flattened organizations and empowered employees – just as many of you find your own businesses. *(5)*

But perhaps our most dramatic achievements have been through the innovative use of advanced technologies. From the drill pipe in our wells to the tail pipe of your vehicles, technology is transforming this business.

For example: in our upstream business – the exploration and production of oil and natural gas – we've made fantastic advances in determining where our best chances of success are before we drill. We've reduced the risk of drilling dry holes; and that drives down our costs.

The key has been the development and application of three dimensional seismic imaging. We've long used reflected sound generated by explosives or other sources to give us a two-dimensional view of the earth's layers below the surface.

3D seismic coupled with sophisticated, computer-enhanced processing opens new vistas. Now the resolution is much greater, to the extent that we can see folds and traps in the subsurface where petroleum can be expected to accumulate that were obscured or hidden by the limits of 2D seismic. *(6)*

We're also improving our techniques for generating this information. Initially, we could use 3D seismic only in open water, or dry, easily accessible land. But with the use of hydroplaning marsh boats and sophisticated telemetry, we now take 3D seismic into swamps and marshes – environmentally sensitive areas *(7)* – and gather data affordably and responsibly.

Harnessing breakthroughs in computer technology initiated in the aerospace and defense industries, we've increased our ability to extract more information about the type of rocks and fluids which lie thousands of feet deep into the earth. *(8)*

There have been equally as significant advances in drilling and production techniques.

Perhaps the best example here is horizontal drilling, which Texaco and others first developed and applied in the Danish North Sea.

In horizontal drilling, engineers drill vertically, pushing inch-thick steel drill pipe thousands of feet straight down. But, then they gradually turn the direction of the drill bit, reaching a 90-degree angle, bending the pipe until they are boring horizontally through the oil-bearing strata. *(9)*

This exposes more oil – doubling, tripling or even quadrupling the amount we can get from a single vertical well hole. That translates to fewer wells and less investment – an environmental plus and an economic success. *(10)*

Mr Decrane now explained another advance – the quadra-lateral oil well – and what it meant.

The advances don't stop with the opening of new fields.

After we have our wells producing from the reservoirs, there are still many opportunities to maximize efficiencies through the use of technology.

Not too many years ago recovering 20 per cent or less of the hydrocarbons that are trapped in a reservoir was the standard. But, borrowing three-dimensional visualization software from the movie industry *(11)* we are now able to follow on a computer screen the flow of water, steam, carbon dioxide or chemicals that we inject into reservoirs to loosen the hydrocarbons and push them out. These enhanced recovery techniques are increasing by two- to three-fold the number of barrels we now can recover.

This ability to grab technology, not just from our own research, but from any industry – defense, medicine, entertainment – and apply it in creative ways has transformed the petroleum industry and actually increased available supplies of crude oil and natural gas. And it is this same ability that has helped us drive the costs down.

Similar strides in improving both technology and its application are evident in our 'downstream': the refining and marketing of gasoline and other products.

Mr Decrane then listed five examples. Three would have been better if he had wanted his audience to remember them individually. Five drove home the general point that his industry was innovative and environmentally responsible.

So the petroleum industry has a proud record of continually driving down costs, improving quality and growing the available supply. That is how we've been able to survive as an industry that deals in a declining resource commodity whose price is declining in real terms.

The petroleum industry continues to be one of the most important industries in the world today – fundamental to economic prosperity and to the quality of life, both here in our highly industrialized US economy – and around the world.

Reliable, plentiful supplies of affordable, environmentally responsible energy, drive economic growth. Industrial countries use, on the average, 40 barrels of petroleum per person per year. Developing countries use less than five. Those latter countries' ability to grow, prosper and achieve a higher standard of living is directly related to their ability to access affordable energy.

In developing countries around the world we've seen the ugly impact on the environment from the use of such non-petroleum sources as wood, dung and high-sulphur, unprocessed coal. So many of those countries are reaching out for petroleum products. *(12)*

Why petroleum? Because despite all the talk of new, alternative or renewable fuels, there simply is no comparable source of energy that can rival petroleum for economy, abundance, efficiency, cleanliness and safety.

Oh, battery-powered cars are highly touted. But we must remember that even if battery technology is improved, those cars need to be 'plugged in' to be recharged. How would we generate all the electricity needed to charge them? Unless we want to build a lot of new nuclear plants, which is unlikely, that power would have to come from burning oil, gas or coal – from hydrocarbons.

And many who focus on 'alternative fuels' such as compressed natural gas and LPG (liquified petroleum gas) fail to note that they are hydrocarbons furnished by this industry. *(13)*

What about ethanol as an alternative fuel? At best, it is a gasoline extender, not a substitute. It can't compete without government subsidy. Brazil's efforts to use agricultural products as automobile fuels dragged down its economy, and died in a heap.

Ultimately, it should be the consumers who decide which fuel to use and what price they are willing to pay. Today, oil and natural gas provide two-thirds of the energy Americans use, both directly as fuel, and indirectly. The free market continues to choose petroleum as its fuel of choice. That's why the petroleum industry comprises between 3 and 5 per cent of the entire US economy.

It's bigger in terms of output than the automobile industry. And it's bigger than education, social services, computers and computer services, and iron and steel manufacturing, all rolled together. *(14)* It employs 1.5 million Americans in more than 40,000 companies of all sizes.

In the coming years, worldwide demand for oil and gas will continue to grow, particularly in developing countries, such as India, China and across Latin America. Predictions are that the world's current daily consumption of 70 million barrels of petroleum will reach 95 million in just 15 years. To meet this demand and build on it, Texaco and other oil companies are actively seeking new opportunities throughout the world, and applying or developing, exciting new technologies to capitalize on them.

We realize the future of our industry is not entirely in our hands. Whether the oil industry will remain a major asset to the people of the world depends only partly on our companies' demonstrated ability to meet new challenges. I am confident of our ability to continue to innovate and meet the demand.

But, the petroleum industry has a great deal of work to do when it comes to informing consumers about the choices. And frankly this is an area where we have been far less innovative and successful than we have been in handling other parts of our activities. It's something we must change.

Speaking for Texaco, I assure you we are determined to do our part not only to fulfil the energy needs, expectations and demands of the people of the world into the 21st century, but to help the world make informed choices that are good for them and good for the environment. I hope you'll help us to do that. *(15)*"

(1) A quick connection with the audience, and then he tells them what they are going to hear.

(2) After a series of mini-grabbers (gas is cheaper than ever) he delivers two spectacular attention-grabbing comparisons. They also make an early claim on the 'common ground' of being good for the consumer.

(3) Briefly uniting the audience in mockery of a 'common foe' – the invisible experts . . .

(4) . . . who are promptly demolished with three 'killer facts'.

(5) Connecting with his audience again, and flattering them.

(6) The audience may still be mystified by 3-D seismic but they now certainly know what it achieves.

(7) First claim on the 'common ground' of environmental responsibility.

(8) He mentions technologies probably more familiar to his audience and again explains simply what they achieve for his industry.

(9) This conveys a vivid picture – a gigantic drill changing direction. As with other technological references, this would have been a good place for a visual aid.

(10) Another claim on the environmental 'common ground'.

(11) A very well-chosen analogy – everyone in the audience will have watched a movie.

(12) Now he is reaching for the 'common ground' of helping the Third World.

(13) There's a 'killer fact' against the invisible 'alternative fuel' enemy – the alternative fuel turns out to be a hydrocarbon after all.

(14) It is very hard work to convey anything as big as the petroleum industry, but these comparisons give a good general impression.

(15) A final claim on the 'common ground' of consumers and the environment, and then he makes clear how he would like the audience to respond to the speech (help make the case for the petroleum industry).

Graham Allen MP proposing and Tony Wright MP pretending to oppose a Bill in the House of Commons to define the powers of the Prime Minister, 28 November 2001

These excerpts (which I have again stripped of parliamentary circumlocutions) are a study in contrasts, Graham Allen's direct, drawing on history, Tony Wright's playful, heavily ironic, both livened by images and figures of speech. In print, with no guidance as to the speaker's tone of voice, can you be certain that Tony Wright does not mean it?

"Graham Allen: Thomas Paine argued in *The Rights of Man* that 'a government without a constitution is a power without a right'. Power unacknowledged is power unaccountable. Power unbounded is power uncontrolled. *(1)* The time has come for this Parliament to acknowledge and define the true extent of the power of the United Kingdom prime ministership.

We will all be stronger for recognising the central truth of British politics: the office of Prime Minister towers over our democracy. This

mighty oak *(2)* casts a long and chilling shadow over all of us who are drawn close to it, regardless of which party is in office. We all know that there is no political office like it in the democratic world – the concentration of power, the scope of decision making, the span of patronage, the control of both Executive and legislature, plus the informal powers to set the agenda and dominate access to the media.

The development of the office under all incumbents over the past century has made a myth of the notion of parliamentary sovereignty, a lie of collective Cabinet government and a near terminal hollowing-out of our political parties. Our politics, once a rich and varied diet of interaction and competition, has given way to McPolitics *(2)* – a dumbed-down, one-dimensional relationship between a prime min-istership and the insatiable media, with the rest of us reduced to spectators, bit players and cheer-leaders . . . *(2)*

Of course, the office has changed since the time of Walpole, who became the first Prime Minister in 1721 and who spent his day eating Norfolk apples on the Treasury Bench. Each incumbent has added something and the office inexorably continues the trend of accumu-lating power – but that is no force of nature; it is not beyond our con-trol. I propose that we in Parliament stop spectating and make a conscious decision that the evolution has gone far enough – that we define the prime ministership as it is now in law, and that the Execu-tive power should not grow further without the clear consent of this Parliament or a future Parliament. If Parliament does not have the responsibility to draw that line in the sand, *(2)* it has no real purpose at all and our transition to the dignified part of the constitution is complete . . .

Defining the prime ministership does not weaken it and it is not my intention to do that, but neither does my acceptance of a strong Exec-utive imply acceptance of a feeble Parliament. We do not have to choose between the lyrics and the music of our democracy. *(2)* Indeed, being clear about what the prime ministership can do will only help Parliament to rediscover and redefine its own destiny as we are squeezed between devolution, Europe and globalism. It will give us a sustainable role for the future . . .

As the new century begins, knee deep in political cynicism and failing participation, we have a clear and present duty to prepare ourselves for the future and to examine our institutions without exception, however exalted, to ascertain whether they and we measure up. We cannot examine a shadow behind a veil, *(2)* a Prime Minister with unacknowledged powers who is shrouded in the mysteries of an unwritten constitution. Let us now bring our mightiest office out of the darkness into the dawn of democracy, and into the light of the law. *(2)*"

(1) A strong pair and a neat example of anaphora.

(2) This speech is a meteor shower of metaphors. We move from a tree, to a meal, to a theatre, to soldiers refusing to retreat, to a song, to a shadow behind a veil and finally to a dawn. There is enough separation between them to prevent them becoming mixed metaphors.

"**Tony Wright:** Mr Allen is a dangerous man. He has written a seditious tract, which he has been disseminating among a gullible public, and now he introduces a subversive Bill. It may seem innocuous enough. It claims only to constitutionalise the position and powers of the Prime Minister, now to preside over his own Department. The fact that it blows a hole through Cabinet government is the least alarming aspect of what is being proposed. Mr Allens real intention is to engineer nothing less than a constitutional revolution, though he is not honest enough to say so.

He believes that the power of the personal executive has increased, is increasing and should not be diminished but recognised. That is what the Bill would do. That is surely outrageous enough. It makes a mockery of all our preoccupations about whether there are too many special advisers in No. 10, whether the Cabinet Office has been annexed to a Prime Minister's Department and whether Cabinet government is now dead. How dare he mock our concerns in this way? How can we go on warning of the dangers of a Prime Minister becoming a President when Mr Allen has the nerve to suggest that a British

Prime Minister with a secure majority and a unified party already has far more unchecked power than an American President could ever dream of?

But it gets much worse. Mr Allen seems to believe that a system of strong government needs a system of strong accountability. Again, that may sound reasonable, but does the House understand that it means an end to Parliament as we know and love it? We would have to stop being happy hamsters on a wheel and become eager beavers, required to think for ourselves in holding the Executive to account and debating the great issues of the day; nobody would write our press releases for us and there would be no collective line to save us the effort of thinking. Instead of representing Parliament to the people, we would have to start representing the people to Parliament.

That only begins to touch on the enormity of Mr Allen's proposals. We depend on the Executive. We may call ourselves a legislature, but we know that our secret dream is to join the Executive; that is what having a job in this place means. We sit by the Executive's table, hoping to touch the cloth and ready to catch any crumbs that fall. We may only become the Parliamentary Private Secretary to a Parliamentary Private Secretary, but that gives purpose to our lives.

Mr Allen wants to deprive us of our dreams; he wants to take nanny away from us and turn us into grown-ups. The House will understand why he has to be stopped. What is all that nonsense about the separation of powers? In the 18th century, we may have told ourselves that that was how our Government worked, but it was the secret of good government. The Americans and others may even have believed it and acted upon it, but we soon took the precaution of abolishing it. The ultimate wisdom of that course stands revealed in the glories of a supine Parliament and a passive people. We believe in strong, unchecked and unencumbered government, which has taken all the old prerogative powers of the Crown and kept them for itself. That has given us the most concentrated system of unchecked power of any democracy in the world, and we love it.

We pride ourselves on our strong Government; we believe in the idea of winner takes all as long as we are the winner. We do not intend to share power with anybody, certainly not a second Chamber. We like things the way they are; we like to be able to talk about the glory of parliamentary sovereignty while having the convenience of the Executive exercising it for us. If the Executive invite us to abolish habeas corpus in, say, an hour or an afternoon, we are happy to oblige. If they are kind enough to fix the membership of our Select Committees for us, it would be churlish to want to do that for ourselves. We may sometimes say that we would like things to be different, but the truth is that we need our comfort blanket and do not intend to give it up lightly.

Now the Bill wants to take us back 300 years and sever Parliament's dependency on the Executive. It does not have the courage to propose a written constitution, which is the inevitable end of the process. Fortunately, knowing the House of Commons as I do, I am confident that it will prefer to cling to the apron strings of Executive power and have nothing to do with my Hon. Friend's dangerous and subversive Bill. **"**

Sir David Ramsbotham, former Chief Inspector of Prisons in England and Wales, speech to the Prisoners' Education Trust, April 2002

This is a heavily condensed version of a speech which was a model of how to address a well-informed sympathetic pressure group. It is firmly organized around three clear themes and packed with content. The full text can be obtained through the Trust from their website:

information@prisonerseducation.org.

These excerpts show a 'killer fact' delivered with such subtlety that you may not even notice it.

"They say that soldiers can only do things in threes, including thinking. To prove that absolutely correct, there are three things that I want to say, in connection with an overriding message. The message is that of all the things done with and for prisoners, the most important for them, and the one that has the most impact on their likelihood of reoffending, is education. For once both statistics and common sense are in agreement with this!

That message is so abundantly clear that it ought to determine how education is approached with prisoners, but sadly that is not what happens. The three things I want to talk about are the lack of strategic direction, the lack of assessment and the lack of provision. The fact that I have said all this before is a sadness. It suggests that despite all the promises, all the rhetoric, all is still not well with the delivery of education in prison.

When we inspected Ford Prison in September 2000, I was very concerned to be shown a letter from Judith Williams, then acting Head of Prison Education and Skills training, containing the following words: 'Establishments have been set Key Performance Targets in literacy and numeracy at Level 2 in order to achieve the Key Performance Indicator. All Level 2 qualifications in literacy and numeracy achieved in prison count, regardless of discharge dates or screening test results.' (1)

In other words, what mattered was not improving the educational skills of prisoners but achieving whatever target had been set. PhDs could count towards Level 2 figures, provided that they sat screening tests. I described this as cynical and unworthy of the Prison Service.

I don't know whether you are listening to the current series of Reith Lectures by Onora O'Neill, Mistress of Newnham College, Cambridge. (2) In them she pours scorn on the League Table and target-driven culture which infects so many of our public services. No one is guiltier of this than the Prison Service, but I do not blame them entirely. They lack precise direction about what they are to do with prisoners, and so have fallen back on exact compliance with rules and regulations, conformity with budgets and achievement of targets and performance indicators as the goals. Of course, all these are important but they are tools of the management trade not gods in their own right."

Sir David then described the strategic direction which he wanted ministers to give to the Prison Service and why, and the assessments which ought to be made of each prisoner's health, personality, skills and educational ability on arrival in prison.

"And so I come to my third point, provision. You may remember that to his intense embarrassment I quoted the figures given by the Prisons Minister to the House of Commons about financial provision for education. Brinsford gave £482 per young offender per year, Werrington £1,750, Thorn Cross £2,450 and so on. The point is that the money allocated was not based on an assessment of need. It was based on historical figures, subject to the plusses and minuses of additions and cuts, made by individual Area Managers. Not only is vocational training being cut, but the education that goes with it. I will not comment about the Arts other than to wish that the Director-General would stop referring to them as 'recreational training', a demeaning phrase. It has an immense amount to contribute as a trigger and as provider of self-esteem.

Talking of self-esteem I shall never forget a comment made to me by the Governor of the Young Offender Institute at Shotts. He said that if, by chance, he had to get rid of all his staff, the last one out of the gate would be his speech therapist, because of all she did to encourage self-esteem, the essential precursor to further education and training. I took one with me into Swinfen Hall. And her findings?

- 50 per cent of inmates were suffering from some form of substance-induced memory loss, the substance blamed being cannabis.
- 17 per cent had hearing difficulties.
- 37 per cent had severe literacy problems.
- All had significant difficulties with speech, language, and communication, compared with 1 per cent of the normal population.

When I add to them the 65 per cent of adult males with a reading age of less than 8, I feel that provision is woefully inadequate for the needs of those in prison . . ."

(1) Quoting the letter gave Sir David a chance to share his contempt for the jargon and reinforced his identification of the author as a 'common foe' for himself and the audience.

(2) A shrewd connection with the audience, since Sir David had rightly identified them as likely followers of the (high-minded) annual Reith Lectures.

Did you spot the killer fact? The reference to cannabis. With a generally liberal-minded audience there was an 'invisible enemy' (to Sir David) of people who wanted to legalize it. His linkage of cannabis to memory loss in prisoners gave the audience a distinct shock, particularly because it came out of nowhere, in a long aside.

Jon Moynihan, Chairman of PA Consulting Group Consultants, welcoming new recruits to the company 2002

This is the opening of a welcome speech to new recruits to a management consultancy. It ignores several pieces of advice in this book. In particular, it contains some jargon words which were mocked in Chapter 10 and has a list of five instead of three. However it does follow, very well, the basic rules of connecting with the audience and holding a conversation with them. Consultants really use words like 'client-focused' and 'team-oriented'. And they can remember five things on a list, not just the normal three.

"Hi everybody. The last couple of years have shown, through a series of turbulent events, how all of us, as never before, have to keep on our toes regarding what works and what doesn't work, and what kind of consulting firm will succeed, in today's environment. The dot com boom; the dot com bust (1); the telecommunications bust; the tragic events at New York's World Trade Center, all underline that the world we live in, both in business and generally, is a hard and demanding one, with the capacity to surprise and challenge as never before.

At PA, we have survived these rapid and sometimes devastating changes in the world, and even – so far – flourished in that environment, because of a set of values that we believe are right in themselves, and right for PA. I would like to conclude your welcome day with a brief statement of those values, so that you can think about them, watch your colleagues at PA live those values, and deliver on them yourself, as you work and prosper at PA *(2)*.

What are these values?

For shorthand purposes, given that I have only ten minutes of your time, I would sum up the 'perfect consultant' in five phrases:

First: client-focused

Second: selfless and team-oriented

Third: ethical

Fourth: commercially-driven *(3)*

Fifth: seeking to excel.

The first of these, **client-focused**, is the most important. All that a consulting firm is made up of is a group of consultants, supported by a bunch of administrative staff. All these people are there to do is to serve the firm's clients as best as they possibly can. That is what we're paid for. That is our raison d'être as a firm. If any consultant does not like being with clients – talking client, dreaming client, obsessing client *(4)* – then that consultant should not want to be at PA. If our consultants are not prepared to put the interests of the client ahead of their own personal interests, they will not be successful at working with clients. *(5)* We don't want such people at PA.

That's not a problem at PA, because a client focus is deep in the value systems of all of our consultants – they are here to serve the client, and they will do whatever it takes to make our clients successful. **'Client-focused'** is our number one value, and PA is looking to you to make sure that that value shines out of you, *(6)* whoever you are, whatever you do at PA, for as long as you are with this company.

The next value I have described in the phrase **'selfless and team-oriented'**. Consultants as a breed are individualists. They have to be, because they need to be creative and brilliant and they need to stick to their beliefs when all around are doubting those beliefs. But, consultants who translate this individualism into acting solely as lone wolves won't build a great consulting firm. Unless we all work as a *team*, so as to make the output of the team greater than the potential output from its individual parts, PA will never be more than but a collection of gifted individuals, who are setting out eagerly on the road to failure *(7)*...**"**

(1) A common and effective technique – yoking together something and its opposite as having the same characteristics (A and Not-A are both B). It makes B more memorable.

(2) Telling them particularly clearly what they are going to hear.

(3) Three bits of hyphenated jargon in a row would not work for an everyday audience: in this context they go straight to the point.

(4) An excellent trio.

(5) The key word 'client' is deliberately repeated, like a litany or mantra.

(6) Perilously close to cliché but the simplicity of the image works well here since it contrasts with the abstract concept of 'client-focused'. (A pedant would object that a focus cannot shine out of anything, even a consultant.)

(7) A dramatic paradox, creating surprise and making listeners think.

Index

HIGH IMPACT COMMUNICATIONS

Books to make you better at getting your messages across...

Read This
Robert Gentle
0273 656503

Information overload. Everyone has too much to read. So, what's going to make people read what you write? Simple, clear, commanding writing – that's what. Here's how.

Powerwriting
Suzan St Maur
0273 659065

Most business writing books teach you how – but to succeed you need to learn what to write, too. That's Powerwriting – your key to winning words!

That Presentation Sensation
Martin Conradi
0273 654748

For the presenter, a presentation can be a make or break, career-turning experience. This inspirational book shows you how to be unforgettable – packed with advice and ideas from leading business people who already are.

Available at all good bookshops and online at
www.business-minds.com